YOUNG ARCHITECTS 5

INHABITING
IDENTITY

YOUNG ARCHITECTS 5
INHABITING IDENTITY

FOREWORD BY MARK ROBBINS
INTRODUCTION BY ANNE RIESELBACH

FORSYTHE + MACALLEN
STEVEN MANKOUCHE
LISA HSIEH
STELLA BETTS
BEN CHECKWITCH
MIKE LATHAM

PRINCETON ARCHITECTURAL PRESS, NEW YORK
THE ARCHITECTURAL LEAGUE OF NEW YORK

Published by
Princeton Architectural Press
37 East Seventh Street
New York, New York 10003

For a free catalog of books, call 1.800.722.6657.
Visit our web site at www.papress.com.

Editing: Jennifer Thompson
Design: Jan Haux

 The publication was supported in part with public funds from the
New York State Council on the Arts, a state agency.

NYSCA   Additional support provided by the LEF Foundation

Special thanks to: Nettie Aljian, Nicola Bednarek, Janet Behning, Megan Carey,
Penny (Yuen Pik) Chu, Russell Fernandez, Clare Jacobson, John King, Mark Lamster,
Nancy Eklund Later, Linda Lee, Katharine Myers, Jane Sheinman, Scott Tennent,
Joseph Weston, and Deb Wood of Princeton Architectural Press
—Kevin C. Lippert, publisher

Library of Congress Cataloging-in-Publication Data
Young architects 5: inhabiting identity/foreword, Mark Robbins;
introduction, Anne Rieselbach.
    p.   cm.
 ISBN 1-56898-458-8 (pbk.: alk. paper)
1. Young Architects Forum. 2. Architecture—Awards—United States.
3. Architecture—United States—21st century. 4. Young architects—United States.
I. Title: Young architects five.
NA2340.Y6794 2004
720'.92'273–dc22
                    2003024804

CONTENTS

ACKNOWLEDGMENTS

Rosalie Genevro, Executive Director,
The Architectural League of New York

The rich content of this publication can be directly attributed to the efforts of the Young Architects who have so thoroughly and thoughtfully presented their work.

Corporate sponsorship is an essential component of the continued quality of the presentation of the Young Architects Forum. The League gratefully acknowledges the support that has made this series and publication possible. Ongoing commitments from A.E. Greyson & Company, Artemide, Dornbracht, Hunter Douglas Window Fashions, Miele Architects and Designers Resource Group, and Tischler continue to insure the success of the Young Architects Forum exhibition, lectures, and web site installations.

This publication would not be possible without the support of the LEF Foundation and the efforts of the staff at Princeton Architectural Press.

FOREWORD

Mark Robbins

I am sitting at a desk in a stuccoed cottage in the woods, looking at a field of prehistorically large ferns and green-quaking Aspens through a gridded wall of windows. It has been nearly fifteen years since I have been to this retreat for artists, where filmmakers, composers, painters, and writers—excised from places like New York, Boston, and Los Angeles—have come to work since the early part of the last century. (Their names are signed on slabs of wood inside each cottage: Aaron Copland, Milton Avery, and, more recently, Joan Semmel and Francesca Woodman.) Some artists now come from fields that were unimaginable one hundred years ago. Though architecture had been part of the original mission of the colony, it had somehow gotten lost. I was one of the first architects in residence then and worked on plans for an installation, a publication, and a series of collages. A lot got done in those eight weeks away from my apartment and studio in Hell's Kitchen; friends called it art camp, but in some respects it was harder than work in the city. The time was clearly limited, and there was no excuse not to produce in paradise.

This summer, not without some accidental poetry, I have been assigned the same studio. The interior has been lined with painted sheet rock, and a battery of fluorescent tubes worthy of Dan Flavin now light the ample white space. The forest has been cut back, extending a rough-hewn axis out to Mt. Monadnock. These days I am working at a monitor with the parallel rule off to the side, scanning and composing images of homes that for the most part look nothing like the iconic rooms we studied in architecture school or the ones we design for others.

Architects, especially younger ones, have few places in which to work apart from the structure of school and client practice, though time like this can mark the broadening of aspirations about theory, drawing, and building. In such a setting, alongside the twelve-tone scores of composers and the abstract stanzas of language poets, experimental, critical work in design has a valued place.

The Architectural League's Young Architects program is the first chance for many recent architecture school graduates to present their work in a public forum. It is the opportunity to consider the existence of a personal body of work and have it debut among colleagues and strangers. Each year's winners became a class of sorts. A poster by Glenn Weiss for the tenth anniversary of the Young Architects series diagrammed, like Hans Haake, the connection between these designers: shared exhibitions, projects, romantic and business partnerships. We were a small circle of mostly New York-based architects; the connections between us were many and varied. I think about them and about where they are now. They are practitioners who have done well, and many have used their training in different ways. They are deans, directors of schools, curators, critics, writers, artists, and teachers. Some have stayed on the East Coast, while others have dispersed to the Midwest, the far West, and abroad.

For the young and mobile designers in this year's Young Architects competition, politics and production meet. Their work on the following pages explores fresh means of dwelling and looking at identity, presenting the material world of building amidst the flux of contemporary life. Rather than chasing an earlier architectural grail of an "autonomous object" or playing uncritically to the market, many of these designers challenge, in concrete terms, received notions about who we are now. For them, complexity comes without direct quotation and with a sense of possibility that disrupts an acquiescence to familiar patterns.

Twenty years ago in his book *The Gift*, Lewis Hyde wrote about the making of art and the difficulty of reconciling art and creativity in a market economy. Art can be traded, he said, but when it becomes only a commodity it is transformed both for the artist and for those who experience it. For architects, focusing only on the source and evolution of creative work may be even more problematic when so much of what we do is clearly about satisfying contractual, practical, and economic needs. Exploration, risk, and a constant reconsideration of work that is not directly related to the market becomes harder to sustain and most often is snuck in at the edges of practice, behind closed doors. Institutional largess can enhance the possibility of independent work by providing time to think and experiment. This ultimately enriches our work. The Architectural League and a notable few foundations and organizations have managed to support and exhibit new work, giving a generation of architects and designers the permission to follow their own lead as well as the recognition that it matters. Now in its twenty-second year, the Young Architects Competition continues to identify designers of remarkable talent who will challenge perceptions of what architectural practice can be.

MARK ROBBINS is a recipient of the Rome Prize from the American Academy in Rome, grants from the National Endowment for the Arts and the Graham Foundation and artist fellowships from the New York Foundation for the Arts. A monograph on his work, *Angles of Incidence,* is published by Princeton Architectural Press. Robbins was director of design at the National Endowment for the Arts, where he undertook an aggressive program to strengthen the presence of innovative design in the public realm. Previously, he was an associate professor in the Knowlton School of Architecture at The Ohio State University and curator of architecture at the Wexner Center for the Arts.

INTRODUCTION

Anne Rieselbach

Inhabiting Identity, the theme of the twenty-second annual Architectural League Young Architects Forum, addressed an elemental architectural design problem—individual place making. Participants were asked to analyze their work in relation to a series of questions, which focused on how faster modes of communication and travel have caused us to rethink traditional notions about the relationship between place and identity. Among the questions posed were: "Must we inhabit architecture in order to identify ourselves, or do new notions of identity render architecture inconsequential? Inhabiting Identity challenges the notion of habitation as fixed and defined, and seeks to engage its dynamic, transformative, and mutable qualities. How does your work reflect or identify these varied roles and scales of habitation?"

The Young Architects Forum was created in 1981 to recognize and encourage the work of architects and designers beginning their professional careers. Participants are chosen through a portfolio competition announced by a call for entries each fall. Entry requirements are loosely outlined, "young" not defined as an age but rather by career location–ten years or less out of undergraduate or graduate school. Winners are chosen not for the size of their design portfolio or the extent of their built work, but instead for a clear design vision and voice, with an eye to represent within the group of competition winners the varied scope of young practices. The six winners are then given the opportunity to expand their presentation, first through an installation at the Urban Center and subsequently in this publication.

This year's competition theme was developed by the Young Architect Committee, a group of past competition winners, in response to the League's program initiative "Habitation," which generated the design ideas investigated throughout the 2002–2003 lecture schedule. The committee also asked prominent members of the design community to serve on the jury. In addition to committee members Andy Bernheimer, Petra Kempf, and J. Meejin Yoon, jurors for 2003 were Shigeru Ban, Wendy Evans Joseph, and Marion Weiss.

Central to each year's competition, the theme is intended as an organizing and editorial tool. Entrants are encouraged to reexamine their own work and to begin to articulate a design philosophy. With its emphasis on how architects create living spaces for themselves and others, this year's theme reflects the work that forms the core of many young architects' practices. Their earliest built work most frequently includes designs for their own living spaces, as well as for family and friends. These commissions embody in microcosm some of the same programmatic concerns as residential projects designed at a larger scale. Distilled to the essential, these smaller projects for dwelling must respond directly and sensitively to the inhabitant's physical, emotional, and intellectual needs, while keeping in mind economic and physical realities.

Winners had the opportunity to revisit the competition theme through their installation designs. Many stretched the potential of the material and design explorations illustrated in their portfolio pages by creating small-scale, three-dimensional structures that both embodied and housed their work. Building these representative samples offered sheltered viewing spaces in an environment, which sympathetically amplified the work illustrated within. No single material or aesthetic prevailed: from recycled wood pallets to glass encased pixels, there was a heterogeneous mix of forms and styles rarely seen in design publications featuring the work of senior architects.

Stephanie Forsythe and Todd MacAllen of Forsythe + MacAllen Design Associates define design's basic requirements simply: " . . . to be warm, dry, and clean, to awaken refreshed, to take in sunlight and fresh air, to gather with others, to contemplate on one's own." The Vancouver firm presented their work in an almost domestic environment. While wall panels held images of some designs, the bulk of the material on display—including project books for their three built houses and a number of recent larger-scale design competitions, models, and a prize-winning tea set and glasses—was set on and in a layered yellow cedar table flanked by two chairs designed by the architects. Nestled in the corner, this arrangement gave a sampling of the materials that comprise their work and an opportunity to examine documentation of the firm's design process.

Constructed of recycled wooden industrial pallets, Steven Mankouche's installation reconfigured the material and form of his Wireless Teahouse designed for the 1999 "Indefinite House" Shinkenchi-ku

Residential Design Competition, later built in Snowmass, Colorado, and reinstalled in St. Louis. The teahouse, like many other young architects' projects, expresses a "nomadic alternative" to traditional forms with its starkly elemental, mutable form. A portfolio of Mankouche's work housed inside the structure included a scheme for the Cleveland Case House Study competition and furniture designs for pieces that transform, move, and otherwise challenge traditional uses. The pieces express the underlying theme of his projects, whether elaboration of the container is essential or whether "the objects that we carry with us from home to home are more about inhabitation than the architecture they lie in."

Lisa Hsieh's ethereal Room Zero, constructed of clear vinyl tubing and acrylic rod, was intended to be "a place for isolation, oblivion, and erasure." Designed to be perceived as a form comprised of "infinite indistinct circles," the projects on display further engaged the idea of lightness programmatically, functionally, and structurally. Included were images of inflatable "urban sleeper" modules (that, when needed, could project from existing building facades for "in-between" zones of the urban fabric) and the almost endlessly reconfigurable N! House. Another project, the Temporary Permanent House (designed for the Thirteenth Takiron International Competition in collaboration with Jr-Gang Chi) was comprised of a permanent structural system combined with a demountable floor and an inflatable wall and roof system held together with stabilizing tensile cord and fasteners.

The design process that informs Stella Betts's architectural work takes "the logic of technological systems and the language of the virtual...into the physical/architectural." Betts, a partner with David Leven in Leven Betts Studio, has designed a number of commercial and residential projects. Her straightforward exhibition design contained six projects vertically displayed on backlit extruded aluminum "sticks." Each stick carried a sliding magnifying lens for closer project viewing. Whether for a printing plant reconsidered as a networked circulation conduit or for a furniture showroom utilizing open glass planes and mirrors to allow multiple viewing points, Betts's minimalist designs contain simple gestures that in turn frame a complex series of spatial and figural juxtapositions. Another built project, a Chelsea penthouse, incorporates a sliding glass screen that both bisects an otherwise spare open space and "re-scales reflected images of the city into a domestic space."

In effect a twenty-first century camera obscura, Ben Checkwitch's folding steel and plexiglas table/screen provided a viewing area for images of his work. Projected images reflected off a preexisting gallery mirror onto the diffused screen surface. A kind of world within a world, with a transformable shape, the installation's imagery aligns with Checkwitch's architectural explorations—notably his Borderless Room. Designed for use in large, open interior spaces, the freestanding, transportable Borderless Room has multiple functions as a lamp, a screen, a storage container, and a bedroom. Closed, its translucent walls glow as an oversized illuminated lantern. Open, its upholstered interior reveals a ventilated body-scaled, basic living space complete with storage and a sleeping area. Theoretically, on the road it could serve as a storage container until reinstalled for use as a living module within a new space.

Mike Latham's work, which ranges in scale from built furniture to projects for houses, is designed with an eye to integrating technology, transparency, and motion. A "technological sculpture" comprised of a glass box encasing a computer-generated slide show, it clearly articulates the components, virtual and real, that characterize the work of his firm Arts Corporation. Latham sees his modular designs as a response to the "growing connections and similarities in space and time" with their ability to acknowledge the "breakdown of the place-specific whole into a series of parts—pliable, reconfigurable, and fluid, like information itself." The resulting versatile forms, such as mobile glass storage closets and room dividers, often serve multiple functions, both dividing and creating space. Another project, HOME.in.1, a six-foot-square, self-contained "home" with storage space as well as sleeping and work areas, provides the owner a small permanent home that can be transported from dwelling to dwelling, as demonstrated by a recent cross-country move.

Much of the work on display exemplified this generation's attempt to mediate the globalization of culture and the continual onslaught of movement and information with the particulars of making place. Whether tailored to the individual body or formed loosely around the inhabitants' singular needs, the designs offer an inventive variety of formal solutions. Although sometimes mutable (and even moveable), the work affirms a connection between body and place. The designs reflect an acute awareness of the need for design strategies to create habitation that touches the ground lightly while at the same time offering a real sense of shelter.

BIOGRAPHIES

Stephanie Forsythe and Todd MacAllen have a multidisciplinary design practice based in Vancouver, Canada (www.forsythe-macallen.com). Both Stephanie and Todd graduated in 2000 from Dalhousie University with their master of architecture degrees. Todd also holds a fine arts degree from the University of Victoria and a bachelor of environmental design from Dalhousie University. Stephanie studied glass blowing and design at the University of Industrial Arts in Helsinki and Sheridan College in Canada; architecture at Ryerson University in Toronto and Otaniemi Technical University in Finland; and holds a bachelor of environmental design from Dalhousie University. **FORSYTHE + MACALLEN** have received two ar+d awards from *Architectural Review* and the Ron J. Thom Award from the Canada Council for the Arts. They won first prize in a competition to design two hundred units of housing and community facilities at the center of Aomori city, in northern Japan. The competition, judged by Tadao Ando and Jean Nouvel, attracted the attention of four thousand competitors from eighty-six countries. They are currently working on the project for Aomori.

STEVEN MANKOUCHE received his architectural training at Cornell University and the Architectural Association in London. His practice, Atelier Mankouche, established in 1996, focuses on issues of residential design and the fabrication of domestic objects. Mankouche has lectured and taught architecture at institutions in the United States and abroad, including University of Michigan, the State University of New York at Buffalo, and the Fachhochschule Liechtenstein. He has received numerous fellowships and awards including a Willard A. Oberdick Fellowship at the University of Michigan and an Architecture Research Fellowship at Akademie Solitude in Stuttgart, Germany.

LISA HSIEH received a bachelor of science degree in mathematics from National Taiwan University, a master of arts degree in mathematics from Indiana University, and a master of architecture degree from the University of Michigan. She has taught in the Department of Mathematics at Indiana University and worked for Morphosis and Hodgetts + Fung in Los Angeles. She is currently working for Mancini-Duffy in New York City.

STELLA BETTS received her bachelor of arts degree from Connecticut College and her master of architecture degree from Harvard University Graduate School of Design. In 1997 she started Leven Betts Studio (www.levenbetts.com) in New York City with her partner David Leven, who received his master of architecture degree from Yale University.

BEN CHECKWITCH holds an undergraduate degree in environmental studies from the University of Manitoba and a master of architecture degree from Dalhousie University in Halifax, Nova Scotia. Working in Canada, Norway, and the United States, he has worked in the fields of construction, naval architecture, and architecture. In New York he has worked for Rafel Viñoly Architects and is currently employed by Gluckman Mayner Architects. He was the recipient of the Rosetti Scholarship in 1997 and was awarded Design Distinction in *I.D.* magazine's 2003 Annual Design Review. He founded Ben Checkwitch Design (www.check-witch.com) in 2002.

MIKE LATHAM is the principal and founder of Arts Corporation, a New York-based design firm interested in the intersections of architecture, art, and technology. Since 2000, Arts Corporation has worked on a diverse range of projects including buildings, interior design, and furniture. The firm has also created a noteworthy body of artwork, principally sculptures and robotics. Mike Latham received his bachelor of arts degree from Columbia College and his master of architecture degree from Columbia University, where he has also taught.

FORSYTHE + MACALLEN DESIGN

Our first built houses, shown here, represent a response to the contemporary human condition, which we feel is often artificial and physically disengaged.

We built these houses. We drew the plans directly on the land, cut and milled lumber from trees felled on the site, made design improvisations as new information, insight, and material were revealed. We experienced the slow turning of seasons, first light, and the subtleties and extremes of weather. This represents a fundamental part of our ongoing education—a need for ideas to pass from our minds to our hands and back again, ingraining a sense of materiality, making, physical space, and experience. As a result, we think it is possible to move into a clearer understanding of space making. In our more recent work we reflect on this experience, allowing ourselves to be more abstract, removed, and analytical. We balance back and forth between abstraction and an intimate relationship with site, material, and construction.

Our first projects have been rural. Like many people we are drawn to the two extremes of the city and the rural landscape. We have searched for ways to engage both urban housing and public space. In particular, urban housing that contributes to the public space. Every time you make a house in the city, you are also making the city itself. We are interested in intensifying the experience of nature in daily urban life. We want to see better-quality construction via prefabrication and design become the norm. These are the main ideas underlying our competition-winning scheme for Aomori, Japan.

MACALLEN HOUSE

This is our first built project—a full-time residence for Todd's parents. The house is on a small island off the west coast of British Columbia, a lush and beautiful landscape of ocean, mountains, and rain forest.

For most of the winter the skies are overcast and gray. One of the main considerations for the house was the creation of a large, open, and light-filled space that flows between and is defined by the volumetric solids of the hearth, guest rooms, and service spaces. The central support for the house is the hearth, which we built from locally collected granite till, deposited on the island by retreating glaciers. No two stones are alike. Wood that we salvaged from the family's old cabin on the site was used to make wardrobe cabinets for the guest rooms and the bridge, which crosses over to those rooms. The house was set back into the hillside to reduce its mass and connect the upper and lower levels of the site. Winter's gray and gentle light enters the building from above and from the sides through a lattice of wood and glass. The light is warmed as it bounces off wood surfaces of Douglas fir, elm, and maple. The resulting warm glow gives one the feeling that the sun is about to break.

1

2

3

4

5

6

1 Vaulted ceiling in main space
2 Deck off of den
3 Stair

4 Elevation photo
5 Study model
6 Front elevation drawing

7

8

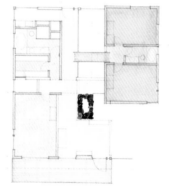

9

7 Main space
8 Ground plan
9 First floor plan

10 Front elevation at night

GALLERY HOUSE

We built this long narrow house for an artist and a teacher. It consists of a series of rooms arranged along a hallway with a gallery on one side and library on the other. The plan was drawn on-site to follow the shape of a natural stone plinth; the resulting rectilinear plan is slightly kinked and tapered. The form is perceived in the gallery/hallway as a transition from the public part of the house to the private. The form, punctured only by a few select openings on its western side, also affects views and the way natural light enters the house. Sunlight bounces off wood and white plastered surfaces, rendering soft, indirect light onto the artwork. Splashes of reflected color (yellow, blue, green, pink, and violet) also light the walls and floor, depending on the time of day and season. The Douglas fir timbers that make up the exposed roof structure and rain-screen cladding were horse-logged and milled on-site with giant yet remarkably nimble Clydesdale horses. The yellow cedar floor was salvaged from a local tennis court. It was stacked and ready to burn when we found it. By milling one-eighth of an inch off the weathered face, the pol-ished, buttery yellow surface of the cedar is revealed. The floor reflects a warm, sunlit glow, even on the most overcast days. In the summer the house is opened to the public for exhibitions. Large doors open onto exterior decks, enlarging the floor area.

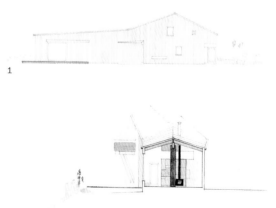

1

2

3

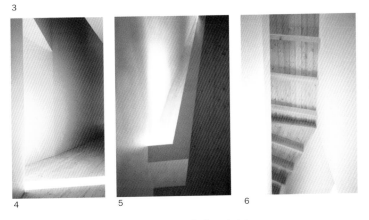

4

5

6

1 Elevation drawing
2 Section

3 Ground plan
4 Gallery hallway
5 Reflected light makes color
6 Ceiling in gallery hallway

7   Main bedroom, natural light from below
8   Main beam in bedroom:
    images 6–8 show continuity of the ceiling structure throughout the house
9–10 Gallery hallway

COLORADO HOUSE

This small house was designed for a woman and her horse. It is in the rolling landscape of the foothills to the Colorado Rockies at eight thousand feet above sea level. There are no other signs of habitation anywhere in sight. Our client is very much on her own.

The building is almost iconographic; it gives warmth from a distance. One could be approaching in the evening, during a snowstorm, and the house reaches out, offering comfort. In this way it is like the myth that reoccurs in many cultures—a story told many times where a traveler, tired and cold, sees a light and a house.

The house opens to the south, gaining a distant view across the meadow, a steward of the landscape. To the north, the house is protected from harsh northern weather by a large outcropping of granite. The ridge of the roof is spread open to bring a slice of the big, colorful, ever-changing southwest sky into the central space of the house.

The house collects and stores radiant solar heat and solar energy.

1

2

1 Study model, photo: Peter Bogaczewicz
2 Ventilation diagram

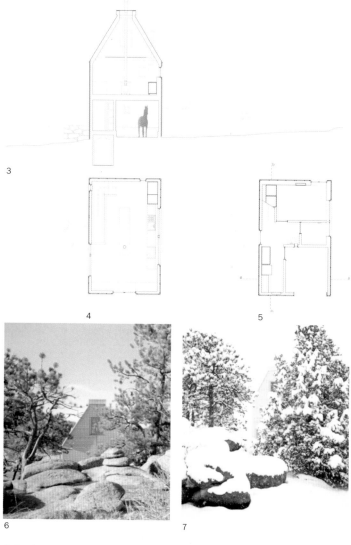

3

4 5

6 7

3 Section
4 First floor plan
5 Ground plan
6 Rock outcrop
7 In snow

8 Elevation

WOOD SHED

This pavilion, surrounded by old-growth fir and cedar trees, was designed to accommodate firewood stored at various moisture levels. Freshly split wood dries quickly when both sides of the end grain are exposed. The shed touches the ground lightly, minimally disturbing the rainforest floor. The parts of the structure that touch firewood or the structure that is near the ground has been scorched and tarred to deter rot-causing organisms. We created the thin, rigid, roof by bending plywood over the frame and fastening it to a temporary support. Consecutive layers of plywood were then bonded with waterproof glue and short screws. When the laminate was cured the temporary support was removed, revealing a simple, light shell. All lumber was site milled from local, selectively horse-logged Douglas fir. The secluded pavilion brings the owners into a part of the property—only a few meters from their home—that they would otherwise rarely visit.

1

2

1 Elevation
2 Drawings

TOOL SHED

This little building was designed and built to contain a small tractor and garden implements. A necessity for fuel storage led to the design of ventilation gaps between the Douglas fir siding boards. The cladding was scorched and tarred. The building's black sheen retains a visible pattern of wood grain and reflects color from the natural surroundings (green, blue, and yellow). Daylight enters through the gaps between the siding and the transparent UV-resistant polycarbonate roof.

1

2

3   4

1 Side and roof
2 Shed in context
3 Detail of charred cladding and corner post
4 Drawings

RESTAURANT

in a Rural Landscape, competition entry

The traditional Japanese house embodies many modernist ideas: free-flowing space, implied rooms, flexible plans, standardized construction, lack of ornament, economy of material, lightness, environmental responsiveness, transparency, a blur between outside and in, etc. Contemporary Japanese architecture recognizes the links between modernism and tradition. It further explores traditional qualities through layered and nested spaces, which have distinct relationships with nature and context. We have designed this rural pavilion as a study of these ideas. Translucent glass cylinders, encircling wasabi gardens, slide up and down. Two layers of glass screens wrap around the balcony space.

1

2

1 Interior and exterior
2 In context

TOMIHIRO MUSEUM

Competition Entry

The Tomihiro Museum of Shi-Ga is a pilgrimage of sorts for the many people who come not only to see the beauty of Azuma Village and the dignity and gentleness of Tomihiro's paintings but also, through his work, to affirm their belief in the importance of simple and unpretentious living. It is a place that inspires courage and joy. The new museum must strive to celebrate these things to the greatest extent possible. Our design intended to quietly make space in the spirit of, and for, Tomihiro's work while maintaining and rejuvenating the dignity and beauty of the site. Three main ideas were our focus: interaction with the land, quiet, gentle gallery spaces, and community.

1

1 Site plan drawing

2

3

Gallery—An ethereal sense of gentle energy is created within the museum by washing the spaces in layers of soft light. A series of fluid, transitional spaces reflect back to the landscape.

4

Community—The new museum is intended to be an important place within the community of Azuma Village. It is a place of pride and inspiration, and it offers a public gathering space, studios for painting and study, and a small theater space in which to enjoy performances.

5

Land—A path through the land is essential to the experience of the museum. The museum forms a bridge between the water and mountain once cut off by the highway. The gallery spaces offer new perspectives of the surrounding nature.

6

CASE STUDY HOUSES

This ongoing series of housing case studies, in a sense, all belong to one project. We think the house can be the root to any building program and that the idea of the house is of primal and contemporary importance.

Within the houses, the main idea is simple; provide an open, flexible space with abundant fresh air and sunlight. In the city, the challenge is to provide this together with the dignity of privacy.

The open spaces are complimented by private, enclosed-dense spaces such as sleeping rooms, washrooms, and services.

On one level there is a very pragmatic idea about borrowing space between indoor and outdoor rooms and between public and private areas, of condensing services and maximizing open, spacious living areas. On a conceptual level it is about a complimentary, reciprocal relationship that emphasizes the spatial qualities of both open and dense space.

Our case studies approach the idea of habitation in a universal way. We design a set of ideas and systems rather than one ideal house. In this way the ideas could then be applied selectively, in various combinations, to different locations and circumstances. We see construction of these houses as an act of assembly rather than an act of building. By separating the house into clear elements it is possible to provide alternatives and site/situation-based improvisations and variations on those elements.

1

2

3   4

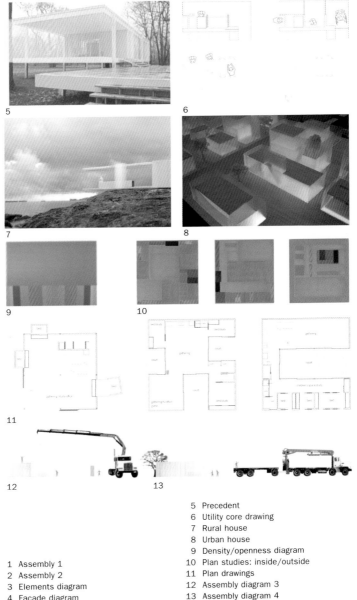

5 Precedent
6 Utility core drawing
7 Rural house
8 Urban house
9 Density/openness diagram
10 Plan studies: inside/outside
11 Plan drawings
12 Assembly diagram 3
13 Assembly diagram 4

1 Assembly 1
2 Assembly 2
3 Elements diagram
4 Facade diagram

AOMORI NORTHERN HOUSING

Three luminous volumes, containing two hundred houses, float in privacy above the active street, defining an outdoor room in the city. This public room is a garden composed of a hill and a pond. At street level an arcade, protected by the hovering housing volumes, encircles the pond and provides access to shops, restaurants, and the first floor of the art gallery. Within the garden, set out on the water, like a cave protected by a low sloping grassy hill, is a large space for daily community activity, seasonal events, and festivals. This setting on the pond emits a play of light, which is reflected off the surface of the water and is viewed like a stage from the street and plaza. In summer the pond creates a quiet, tranquil space in the midst of the busy city. In winter, as a thick blanket of snow mutes the city, the space reverses transforming the pond into a frozen plaza for skating and festivals. The hill becomes a snowy place for children to play and sled, and ramps ascend up to the second floor just outside of the art gallery and children's daycare. This second level also houses a daycare for infants and a day house for the elderly. Deeper into the cave, under the hill, is an auditorium for small recitals and lectures as well as a public bath.

The housing volumes are clad with a double-glass skin. The inner layer, made of sliding glass panels that open onto balconies, transforms each house into a spacious airy terrace. The outer skin is composed of large, vertical, glass louvers made translucent. The large air plenum (balcony space) between the louvers and sliding glass panels ensures that households are well insulated from extremes in hot and cold weather. The louvers mediate the elements. They can be rotated to let in the city and pure light, or to adjust the view. They also form an excellent acoustic buffer, allowing one to be completely removed from the city's activity.

A fundamental idea here is to give shape and identity to the public realm with the fabric of housing. At night the housing volumes become meaningful light sources, floating lanterns in the city. The gentle vigor of individual houses is read, particularly at night, behind the diffuse glass surfaces. From the outside the otherwise still surface of the softly glowing glass volumes becomes rippled in random yet rhythmic, ever-changing patterns of color, light, texture, and motion as banks of windows are pivoted from within individual houses. As one person opens his louvers to let in the cool night air, another closes hers in order to be removed from the city. Within a few balconies futons are hung to air out. Some balconies have white wash hung to dry while several others are enlivened with colorful laundry. The element that veils the diversity between people also reveals that energy.

At both the scale of the city and the domestic interior, relationships evolve between public and private and open and dense spaces.

The apartment's floor area is divided into two clear and rational parts. One section encloses a very dense space of storage, services, bath, toilet, and bedroom units. The remaining area—the family's living space and kitchen—is open, flexible, and flooded with natural light and fresh air.

The open and dense parts of this proposal include several elements that can be added or exchanged to follow the needs of a family as it grows or changes. Interchangeable elements follow changes in taste, requirement, and the growth of children and their needs. The house is also designed to change as needed by a family as its members go about their day. Storage pulls out, and bedrooms expand into larger private environments and shrink again to create a larger unified family gathering space.

1

1 Reflecting pond

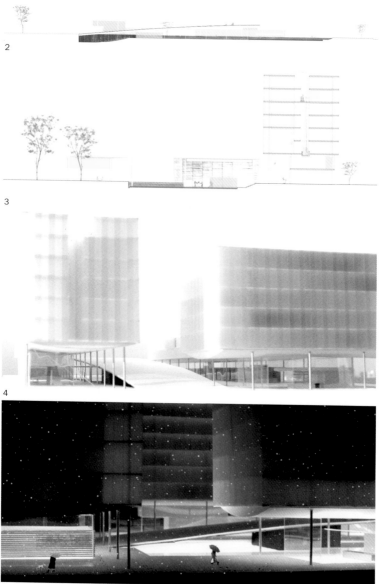

2

3

4

5

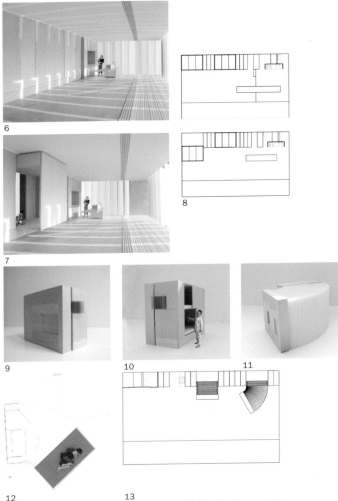

6 Apartment, open space

7 Apartment, private room expanding into
   open space

8 Plan drawings of an apartment

9 Another version of private room, closed

10 Private room, closed with access to bed

11 Private room, open

12 Plan drawing of room, partly open

13 Room in context

2 Section drawing through hill

3 Cross section

4 Hill in between housing

5 Covered walkways at street level

FLOAT: TEA LANTERN

Design studies of the tea lantern began with the idea that a simple object could define a place of gathering. The engagement of the senses, with a quality of light, warmth, and scent, creates an intimate space for gathering or contemplation.

Technically the tea lantern utilizes a double wall, one glass cylinder within another. The space between encloses a vacuum to create a thermal barrier that insulates hot or cold liquids and renders the appendage of a handle unnecessary. (This study is also part of an exploration of building skins that we have been designing.) We used the same principles to design a set of glasses. An inner glass cup, which holds the liquid, is held suspended by an outer glass cylinder (this time without a sealed vacuum space). Aside from insulating, this double skin also serves to elevate the condensation away from the table surface.

Expressively, it is the liquid inside that we wanted to emphasize. There are transparent and translucent variations of the lantern and glasses, in them the tea— or sparkling water, wine, or scotch—becomes a lens of liquid color, suspended in light. If the warming candle is lit the multisensory effect is particularly engaging.

The tea lantern belongs to a series of studies where an object is made with one material only. This represents an attitude toward simplified design and manufacture/construction that we are continually developing. A simplified material pallet, design, and process can lend itself to elegant detailing, economy of labor, and ease of re-use and recycling. In this case the material is borosilicate glass, which differs from the soda lime glass typical of float glass windows, bottles, and such, in that it has an exceptionally high chemical resistance and a negligible coefficient of thermal expansion. The lack of thermal expansion allows for localized heating of the glass at the edge or spot to be fused, bent, slumped, or blown, without causing stress in or distorting the surrounding area of the same piece of glass. The borosilicate glass composition is highly suitable to automated machine processing of glass tubing into vessels with extremely precise dimensional tolerances. These same thermal properties are of course very useful to the finished glass tea set.

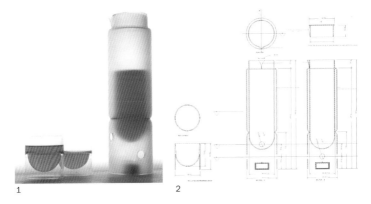

1

2

SLIP JOINT CHAIR

This chair and a display table of similar knock-down construction were designed and made for this exhibition. They belong to a series of objects, which includes the tea lantern, each made from a single material. We attempt to refine and dissolve detail in order to emphasize the material in a pure way. The chairs and table are dry-assembled from flat boards using precise friction fit joints—without fasteners or glue. They may be hung as panels on a wall when not in use or packed flat for shipping.

The chairs and table are made from yellow cedar, which is similar to the Japanese Yellow Cypress and found on the west coast—at mountain foothills—from Washington to British Colombia and to Alaska. It is the hardest of the cedars and extremely resistant to weather and insects. We have left these pieces natural (without oil finish). The wood has a pungent, spicy fragrance similar to the mossy floor of a mature forest after heavy spring rain.

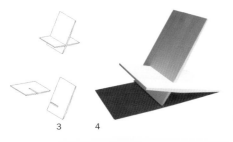

3   4

1 Diffuse glass version with hot tea
2 Drawing of float and cups
3 Drawing of chair
4 Photo of chair

STEVEN MANKOUCHE

Are our homes like our clothes, used as a wrapper to express ourselves to society? If that were the case, would the fashion industry be comparable to the housing market? And where does that leave those who cannot afford high-street designer clothing? What about those who are not fortunate enough to have a house of their own or who have chosen not to? How can they express themselves? Aren't the objects that we carry with us from home to home more about inhabitation than the architecture they lie in?

House Case Study Cleveland tries to propose an alternative to the "haut couture" homes that are built for an elite class. Not unlike a car, the house breaks down into components that are assembled by a variety of ready-made industries. The solution proposes a dry fit house whose components can be altered, reordered, upgraded, or reconfigured within a larger industrial frame. This architecture in a sense challenges the fixed nature of many existing housing types.

Glass House is divided by a furniture datum that hosts most social interactions. The house can be inhabited on both sides of this datum by neighbors, siblings, couples, or strangers; it is mutable and can transform to the inhabitant's needs for space or privacy. The house is transparent, yet privacy is achieved through the use of glass. The more glass that is added as a barrier between people, the more luminosity is lost and opacity through refraction is achieved.

Wireless Teahouse is a reaction to society's fixation on technology. This house is for someone that wants to escape the rigidity of living in an infrastructurally dependent society and proposes a nomadic alternative. It uses the metaphor of the teahouse as a way of commenting on consumer culture. The wireless teahouse is far from really being a house, yet proposes perhaps something closer to architecture: the ceremony of inhabitation.

Domestic objects are often the things that define our personal history. They can be used to speak more precisely at times about the way we inhabit than the house we live in because they have been deliberately chosen. How often in our cities is the architecture we occupy a residual decision of what is available on the market? The objects we rest our bodies against, the ones we have bothered moving, our heirlooms, perhaps, reflect us best.

Through the development of these projects, I hope to cast a different light on the unquestionably accepted elements of living and common objects of our life. Perhaps by affecting what is already with us, like our furniture, our waste products, or our habits of living we can affect the identity of architecture more profoundly than what a different kind of wrapper might express.

HOUSE CASE STUDY CLEVELAND

Spaces Gallery, a collaborative project with James Rayburg and the help of Christian Aldrup

...while "big name" designers are of recognized quality (and will continue to make the sector's "haute couture"), there is a need today for a new kind of individual habitat which, without renouncing quality or a certain contemporary formal expression, would thus become a viable and "available" product for a new kind of consumer demand.
—Peripheriques, *36 Propositions for a Home*

House Case Study Cleveland was a nationally juried show at Spaces Gallery in Cleveland, Ohio. We were solicited to design a house for an invented client on an existing lot in urban Cleveland with a maximum budget of $180,000. The clients were a male couple with two adopted children. One of them was a fireman and car collector, the other was a graphic designer that worked at home and required a home office with a separate entrance.

Looking at the California Case Study Houses built in the 1950s and 1960s, the design principals behind the production of the homes was often guided by an attempt to negotiate the development of a contemporary way of living with the advancements in construction technology. The technology developed at the time reflected the postwar industry of the region that had moved into the civilian consumer market.

Today in Cleveland and around the nation, homes are being primarily built using a construction technology that does not necessarily reflect the technical advancements of the last war. The construction industry never fully applied those developments to the residential market. An industry based on customization finds it difficult to reinvent itself with every project. Hence the methods of fabrication have remained virtually untouched in certain respects, but the management of the production of these products—what we call homes—has been highly developed. The efficiency in the production of components of houses has increased as well.

For Case Study Cleveland, we proposed to tactically use these components of the building industry to produce a "dry assembly" architecture that married a couple of industrial manufacturers (specializing in prefabricated steel building and the custom modular construction) and produce a contemporary expression of living, which was lacking in the Cleveland housing market. Our role in the project was to contain these separate systems and invent an architectural language that closed any potential discrepancies.

A manufactured-steel building spans the site from east to west. After a radiant heated flat concrete slab is poured, the steel is delivered and erected by the steel-building manufacturer. Inserted in this structure are four modular components. These contain private and wet spaces for the residence, which are manufactured in a factory off-site. These spaces or rooms are fully finished with all appliances and fixtures ready to plug in. The house is then sealed with translucent polycarbonate walls, leaving large glazed garage doors that open up the living spaces to the garden. For this reason we pushed our building to the north. The garden becomes an extension of the house—the surfaces become continuous. The garden enters the house. The facade surface becomes the roof and wraps around the back, splitting between the garage and carport, while at the front cradling and advertising the studio space. The entry under this wrapped facade allows one to experience the split between private and public functions of the house.

Just as the two-car garage is the most dominant element in today's track housing, we intentionally exhibited our clients car-collecting hobby in the facade of the house. Not unlike some of his neighbors' display of automobiles on concrete blocks in their gardens, our client can drive his car through the entire structure of the house and publicly exhibit it at the front. In contrast, other areas of the house achieve a high level of privacy through the use of independent rooms constructed off-site. The children's room and office were conceived as plug-in modules with independent climate systems.

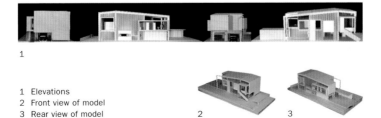

1

1 Elevations
2 Front view of model
3 Rear view of model

2   3

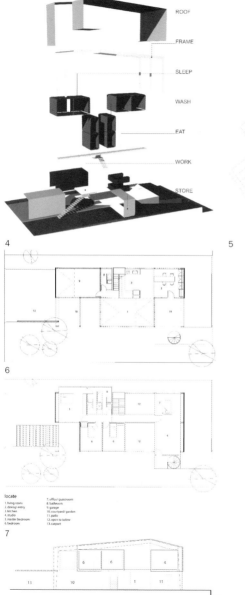

ROOF

FRAME

SLEEP

WASH

EAT

WORK

STORE

4

5

6

7

8

locate

1. living room
2. dining/ entry
3. kitchen
4. studio
5. master bedroom
6. bedroom
7. office/ guestroom
8. bathroom
9. garage
10. courtyard/ garden
11. patio
12. open to below
13. carport

4 Component sequence
5 Site plan
6 First floor plan
7 Second floor plan
8 Cross section
9 "Off-the-shelf" model
10 Folded steel model
11 Grain model
12 Bridging the gap

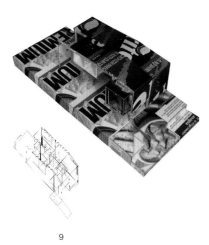

9

Study model expressing the notion of using ready-made systems, branding of different spaces for different uses, and an attempt at making commonly accepted materials precious.

10

Study illustrating continuity of surfaces, exploration of the roof system, and the division of components in the house.

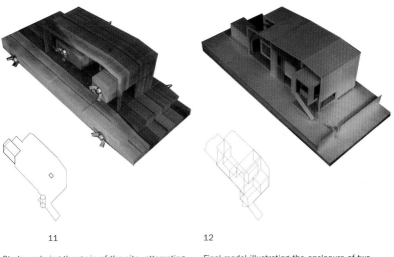

11

Study analyzing the grain of the site, attempting to develop continuous surfaces that relate to the land.

12

Final model illustrating the enclosure of two different systems: modular construction and manufactured steel buildings.

concrete slab/radiant floor heat

stats.

manufact. process:	custom poured
square footage:	2,616 s.f.
$ per sq. ft.	$ 7.42
total cost:	$ 19,410.72

components:	finish:
poured concrete slab	exposed concrete (1221 s.f.)
2 zonal water coil	
heated slab (546 s.f.)	

construction matls.:	concrete, copper coining, steel reinf.
construction type:	site work, excavation, foundation and mechanical

locate

sum:

$ 19,410.72

$ 19,410.72

structural steel frame

stats.

manufact. process:	pre-manufactured steel building
square footage:	1,736 s.f.
$ per sq. ft.	$ 9.21
total cost:	$ 15,988.56

components:	finish:
2 bay steel frame	painted
2 openings per side wall	
steel cross beams at front	
1:12 slope roof	

construction matls.:	structural steel
construction type:	steel

locate

sum:

$ 15,988.56

$ 35,399.28

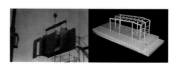

garage

stats.

manufact. process:	standard framing
square footage:	308 s.f.
$ per sq. ft.	$ 37.16
total cost:	$ 11,445.28

components:	finish:
interior wall	insulated type x gwb.
exterior wall	galv-alum corrugated
	metal (722 s.f.)
floor	exposed concrete (see conc. slab)
ceiling	insulated type x gwb.
doors	glass panel garage door, 1 rated standard door
windows	translucent polycarbonate wall (80 s.f.)
heating/cooling	500W electric baseboard

locate

sum:

$ 11,445.28

$ 46,844.56

kitchen/half bath/stair

stats.

manufact. process:	modular
square footage:	364 s.f.
$ per sq. ft.	$ 67.43
total cost:	$ 24,544.52
components:	finish:
interior wall	insulated type x gwb.
exterior wall	OSB
floor	black slate tile
ceiling	insulated type x gwb.
roofing	OSB/finish bamboo flooring (54 s.f.)
doors	1 standard
windows	see enclosure
cabinets	best quality
bath fixtures	toilewt, sink, laundry hook-up: best quality
heating/cooling	500W electric baseboard
stair	wood/bamboo finish

locate

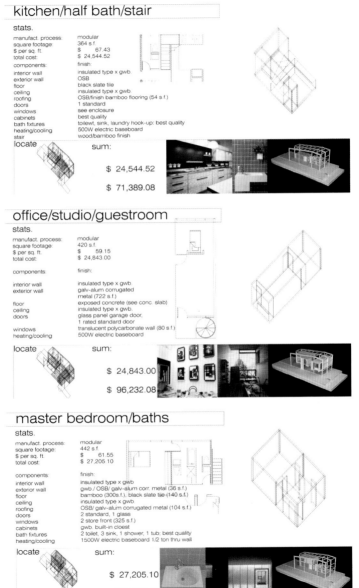

sum:

$ 24,544.52

$ 71,389.08

office/studio/guestroom

stats.

manufact. process:	modular
square footage:	420 s.f.
$ per sq. ft.	$ 59.15
total cost:	$ 24,843.00
components:	finish:
interior wall	insulated type x gwb.
exterior wall	galv-alum corrugated metal (722 s.f.)
floor	exposed concrete (see conc. slab)
ceiling	insulated type x gwb.
doors	glass panel garage door, 1 rated standard door
windows	translucent polycarbonate wall (80 s.f.)
heating/cooling	500W electric baseboard

locate

sum:

$ 24,843.00

$ 96,232.08

master bedroom/baths

stats.

manufact. process:	modular
square footage:	442 s.f.
$ per sq. ft.	$ 61.55
total cost:	$ 27,205.10
components:	finish:
interior wall	insulated type x gwb
exterior wall	gwb./ OSB/ galv-alum corr. metal (36 s.f.)
floor	bamboo (300s.f.), black slate tile (140 s.f.)
ceiling	insulated type x gwb.
roofing	OSB/ galv-alum corrugated metal (104 s.f.)
doors	2 standard, 1 glass
windows	2 store front (325 s.f.)
cabinets	gwb. built-in cloest
bath fixtures	2 toilet, 3 sink, 1 shower, 1 tub; best quality
heating/cooling	1500W electric baseboard 1/2 ton thru wall

locate

sum:

$ 27,205.10

$123,437.18

childrens' rooms

stats.

manufact. process:	modular
square footage:	294 s.f.
$ per sq. ft.	$ 51.17
total cost:	$ 15,043.98

components:	finish:
interior wall	insulated type x gwb
exterior wall	gwb./ OSB/ galv-alum corr. metal (168 s.f.)
floor	carpet
ceiling	insulated type x gwb.
roofing	OSB/ galv-alum corrugated metal (186 s.f.)
doors	2 standard
windows	1 store front (200 s.f.)
heating/cooling	2 500W electric baseboard
	2 1/3 ton thru wall

locate

sum:

$ 15,043.98

$138,481.16

corrugated aluminum roofing

stats.

manufact. process:	steel building maufacturer
square footage:	2898 s.f.
$ per sq. ft.	$ 4.85
total cost:	$ 14,026.20

components:	finish:
roofing	.032 thick galv-alum corrugated metal
ceiling	insulated 2" wood fiber exposed
interior wall	insulated type x gwb.
heating/cooling	ceiling fan

locate

sum:

$ 14,026.20

$152,507.36

enclosure

stats.

manufact. process:	standard framing
square footage:	1334 s.f.
$ per sq. ft.	$ 14.61
total cost:	$ 19,489.74

components:	finish:
interior wall	50% insulated type x gwb., 50% translucent polycarbonate
exterior wall	poli-foil insulation and translucent polycarbonate sheathing
doors	3 glass panel garage doors, 1 store front door
windows	1 store front (100 s.f.), 2 alum. casement

locate

sum:

$ 19,489.74

$171,997.10

carport/stair/bridge

stats.

manufact. process:	custom and pre-manufactured
square footage:	200 s.f.
$ per sq. ft.	$ 20.01
subtotal:	$ 4,002.00
other:	$ 4,000.00
total cost:	$ 8,002.00
components:	finish:
carport:	
frame	steel
wall/roof	.032' thick galv-alum corrugated metal
floor	concrete slab
bridge connector	steel grating
spiral stair	pre-manufactured steel

locate

sum:

$ 8,002.00

$179,999.01

13 Front view from the street
14 Side view from the garden

GLASS HOUSE

Shinkenchi-ku Residential International Design Competition
With the Assistance of Abigail Murray

This project is about questioning the horizon. By laying foundations into the surface of the earth, architecture references the horizon. Most often the ground we walk on serves as a similar constant. Active surfaces, such as the ones we work on, cook on, sleep on, or bathe in change in relation to the ground. What would happen to the architecture if the active surfaces became constant and the ground had to continuously adapt?

Organization

The house is organized around a table running through the center of the house, acting as a datum. This surface also serves as an entrance to the house and is aligned with the horizon, much like Vito Acconci's *Where Are We Now (Who Are We Anyway)* installation. As a result the ground of the house is continuously changing to adjust to the program of this datum. The surface of the dining room table is the same as that of the kitchen counter, which is the same as that of the bed, the bathroom sink, the toilet, and the bathtub. Entering the house is like walking on a runway; sleeping in this house is like lying on the dining room table. Equating the table to the runway in this house makes connections between food, consumption, and fashion. Eating disorders such as anorexia and bulimia commonly present in the fashion industry come to mind when parallels are made among the runway an emaciated model walks on, the surface consumer products enter this house on, and the dining table one eats on.

Diversity

The house is flexible. Two different occupants can inhabit it, one on each side of the table or on each side of the bed. These inhabitants can be roommates or partners. They can share their lives, or they can be neighbors. Communication can occur across the datum line in the center (see scenarios). The rooms can change sizes by sliding glass panels. The house can be open completely to the outdoors. One side of the house is wheelchair accessible. Its plan is determined by minimum slopes in relation to the datum surface height.

Material

The house can be configured for different users. Areas of glass panels that are redundant to multiple configurations become fixed structural blocks that support the roof. Like microscope slides, each glass panel contains information to configure different lifestyles. Privacy in the house is achieved by layering numerous panels of glass, developing opacity through the use of the refractive nature of transparent glass.

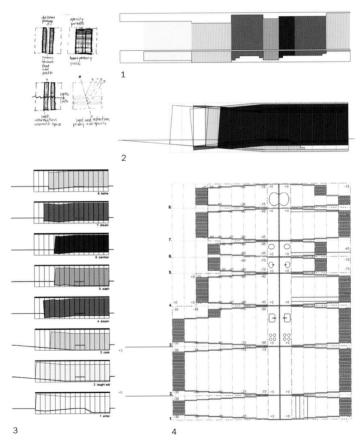

1 Long section: opacity density by program privacy
2 Composite section: opacity core
3 Sections of opacity
4 Generic plan

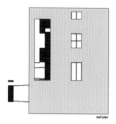

roof plan

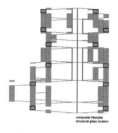

composite lifestyles
structural glass location

single occupancy
old lady with pet

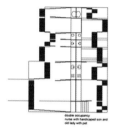

double occupancy
nurse with handicaped son and
old lady with pet

double occupancy
two college students

single occupancy
nuclear family

double occupancy
family with live-in grandfather

double occupancy
retired parents and
musician daughter

single occupancy
artist with live/ work studio

5

5 Different tenant plan scenarios

6 Vito Acconci, *Where Are We Now*,
   (*Who Are We Anyway*)
7 Front view with house open
8 Front view with roof
9 View from rear with house open
10 Front view with house open
11 Side view

6

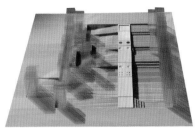

7

8

9

10

11

THE WIRELESS TEAHOUSE

"Indefinite House" Shinkenchi-ku Residential International Design Competition

Just making the box is simple enough; at the outside it takes less than an hour. However, it requires considerable courage to put the box on, over your head, and get to be a box man. Anyway, as soon as anyone gets into this simple, unprepossessing paper cubicle and goes out into the streets, he turns into an apparition of neither man nor box.

. . . Certainly a box man is hardly conspicuous. He is like a piece of rubbish shoved between a guardrail and a public toilet or underneath a footbridge. But that is different from being inconspicuous or invisible. Since he is not especially uncommon, there is every opportunity of seeing one. Surely, even you have, at least once. But I realize full well that you do not want to admit it. You are not the only one. Even with no ulterior motive, apparently one instinctively averts one's eyes. . . .

Why, I wonder, would anyone deliberately want to be a box man?
—Kobo Abe, *The Box Man*

The competition asked participants to reflect upon how technological advances have impacted our living and should thus manifest as changes in our homes. Rather than propose a hardware-intensive house that tied its inhabitants down to a fixed mainframe and infrastructural grid, I proposed a software-based house, the Wireless Teahouse. Taken to an extreme, this vision proposed a dystopian future where inhabitants could choose to alienate themselves from society through the use of technology and live the life of a vagrant, free from the ties of fixed living.

The Wireless Teahouse has nothing electronic. This house has only one assumption: all the technology one needs, the key to all communicative and material needs, can be found in the cellular phone–type device (see ad, p. 62). This permits the house to become a primitive hut where the inhabitant is truly closer to nature. Because of its calculated ritualization of an activity of living—namely drinking tea—the Japanese teahouse becomes a sophisticated prototype for this proposal. The Wireless Teahouse is made entirely of refuse—twenty-eight wood pallets pulled out of the local municipal waste dump or gathered by the street side. The use of the wood pallet in this house becomes synonymous to the format of the tatami mat used for laying out a traditional Japanese teahouse.

The pallets in the Wireless Teahouse are made mostly of oak, a hardwood that constitutes a large percentage of slow-growth, wasted wood resources. These pallets are the unseen tools for moving merchandise and thus a direct product of consumerism. The Wireless Teahouse tries to reflect on the value of technology and the realities of waste. Although promising a life of freedom off the grid, the house still proposes an extremist model where the dweller can choose to be isolated, incognito, anonymous, unknown—a lifestyle that might not be different from that of a vagabond or transient. Looking back at the romantic origins of the tea ceremony, one finds the vagrant Zen monk, who abandoned his opulent life as a prince to seek a way of purity and simplicity in the forest.

More often than not the teahouse is described as the simplest of huts, yet its complexity is derived from its ritualistic use. Is this the point where the hut becomes architecture? The teahouse has two entrances: one at the front for guests and one at the side for the master of the ceremony or the host. Because of the low entrances, the occupants must humbly bow their heads as they enter the teahouse. Upon entering, the guests silently hone their senses, assuming an observational role. They admire a formal arrangement in the *tokonoma*, the quality of light filtering though the space or the sound of frothing green tea as it vaporizes its aroma.

Wandering through the streets of our cities, we have trained our eyes not to take notice of waste: piles of cardboard stacked high at the street's edge, pallets dropped off after a delivery, capsized shopping carts caught with plastic bags, even blinking lights or sirens. To us these large and obtrusive objects have become invisible. Similarly we have made the inhabitants of this wasteland, temporary residents of this landscape, and social deviants invisible.[*] When coming across the Wireless Teahouse, one does not see much more than an inconspicuous pile of wood pallets. Because of its lack of any real fenestration, one can barely notice if it is inhabited at all. Inside the teahouse, the space concerned with ritual is entirely different and focuses on viewing: observing the subtle gestures of the master of ceremony, the inhabitant is surrounded by a play of light and shadow.

One finds that observation, viewing, being viewed, or surveillance plays an important role in the Wireless Teahouse. Like Abe's box man, the inhabitant of this teahouse is safely hidden behind the mask of the pallets yet can easily peer through them onto the unnoticing passersby. In this case freedom comes at the price of being unnoticed. Focusing on the space between the textured wood surface of the walls and what lies beyond, the inhabitant can reach a state of meditation.

Technology has been given an important place in our concerns for future living. As a society we focus a great part of our time looking at monitors or monitoring information. We demand both visibility and invisibility—opposing technological polarities. At these limits we find both: the deviant desire of wanting to observe but not to be seen, and perhaps wanting to be seen but not really observed. At these two extremities we find both the highly craved, refined piece of advanced technological hardware and its unwanted, often discarded soft packaging.

*I am an invisible man. No, I am not a spook like those who haunted Edgar Allan Poe; nor am I one of your Hollywood-movie ectoplasms. I am a man of substance, of flesh and bone, fiber and liquids—and I might even be said to possess a mind. I am invisible, understand, simply because people refuse to see me. Like the bodiless heads you see sometimes in circus sideshows, it is as though I have been surrounded by mirrors of hard, distorting glass. When they approach me they see only my surroundings, themselves, or figments of their imagination—indeed, everything and anything except me.

Ralph Ellison, The Invisible Man, (New York: Random House, 1952)

1

1 Wireless Palm Pilot ad, tree-hugger requesting spongebath.com

2 Teahouse construction sequence
3 Teahouse plans and elevations

2

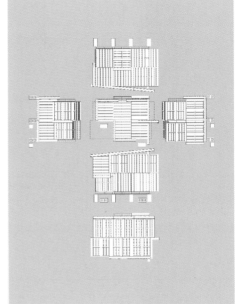

3

Homeless Man Connected to Web

by Scott Jones
The Associated Press

RENO, Nev. – a homeless man was found in a box shelter off interstate 30 surfing the web on a laptop computer. The man, a former CEO and software developer, quit his job 9 months ago and decided to live off the grid.[*]

[*] This article is based on a true story, but entirely fictitious and was never written by The Associated Press nor Scott Jones.

4

5

6

7

4 Teahouse, Andersen Ranch, Colorado
5 Teahouse, nighttime view with projection
   of itself onto itself

6 Teahouse, interior view of guest entrance
7 Teahouse, Artist Guild, St. Louis, "tag-
   ging" graffiti of inner-city youths that
   helped with the installation

DOMESTIC OBJECTS

The following objects attempt to explore notions of function and concept at a different scale. They reflect anatomical analogies, expressions of our body, sexuality, and posture. By questioning a normative understanding of functionality, the objects try to push users to be critical of the conventional use of furniture. We eat on tables. Why can't tables speak of the way we ingest food? If you dislike the food, can your table reject the food?

At a human scale, how do our habits for living—the way we see ourselves—influence our acceptance or denial of objects? Because of their functional identity, the objects of this scale can be effective at questioning commonly accepted cultural notions. These objects normally perform some activity; at times they can lead the user to forget that they, too, are representational or to see beyond their mere use and understand their representational nature.

I like to have a certain level of absurdity, of playfulness, in my work. What sense does it make to have a furniture piece with a single wheel? The object tends to go around in circles when pushed. I try to rediscover the object by reflecting on its nature, its function. A stool with a drain in it: I remember an image of a child peeing his pants and filling his seat with urine. I like my work to make someone do a double-take that paradoxically nudges one out of certainty, complacency, and assumption.

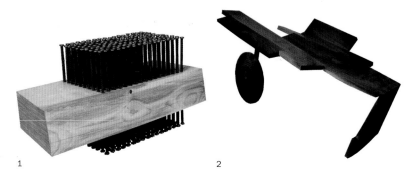

1   2

3

4

5

1 Nail bench
2 Folded table with wheel

3 Cinderblock stool
4 Block stool with wheel
5 Barrel stool with wheel

6

7

8

9

10

11

6 Chair with hole
7 Table for six

8 Mexican hot seat
9 Ken chair
10 Barbie chair
11 Stool with drain

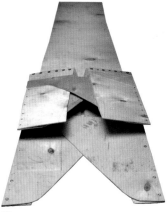

12

13

14

15

12 Aero-ply flattened prototype chair
13 First aero-ply prototype chair
14 Mobile living unit, side view
15 Mobile living unit, view from above   16 Mobile living unit, front view

LISA HSIEH

One day, I dreamed of becoming a carob tree. I was confined to a small circular patch of soil, fenced by bamboo stakes and metal wire. My feet were rooted with my toes planted in the earth. My hair was radiating in fanlike form from my torso. And from the clumped members hung clusters of large dark leathery pods. My mind was numb and my body immobile. With the wind, you could hear the loose seeds rattling in my dangling pods. There is bitterness in being a carob tree: the weight of the large heavy pods, the confinement and immobility. I envied the ever-advancing and mobile world.

The projects presented here consider the ideal of the lightness in living, of mobility, flexibility, possibility, freedom, and liveliness. These projects engage programmatic lightness, functional lightness, operational lightness, and material lightness. The architecture attempts an alliance with a multifaceted and mutable world.

URBAN SLEEPER

URBAN TRILOGY

In-between living*:
In a dense environment like New York City, an affordable apartment is, almost without exception, an undesirable one. Domestic functions are not suitably contained in its single volume, and thus its inhabitants are forced to become city-nomads. They wander endlessly from one place to the next, obscuring the meaning and function of a home.

In-between program:
In-between living undermines the binary of the private and the public and brings about a new urban phenomenon: private activities rendered in public spaces. Certain public programs are endowed with a twofold meaning: while a coffeehouse remains a coffeehouse for some, it is a living room for others. Likewise, a health club is an urban bathroom; a Laundromat, an urban laundry room; restaurants, urban dining rooms. One would not have to stay and pay outrageous rent for an undesirable apartment if it were not for the one missing piece: the urban bedroom.

In-between space:
Despite the congestion of built structures, one place managed to stay intact: the in-between zone (the urban room), which is enclosed/defined by buildings (the inhabitable poché) along the grid streets.

A programmatic analysis was conducted on several blocks within Greenwich Village in New York City. These blocks form an area horizontally defined by streets (from 8th to 14th Street, east/west) and vertically by avenues (5th and 6th Avenue, north/south). Each city block is composed of buildings (the solid, the inhabitable poché) along the grid of streets and of empty space (the void, the urban room) enclosed by buildings. The in-between programs (coffeehouse, health club, Laundromat, restaurants) in the inhabitable poché of the surveyed area were identified and recorded. This analysis revealed a lack of an urban bedroom to fulfill the requirement for in-between living.

With the missing in-between program identified, the objective was to design an urban bedroom and make in-between living feasible. To this end, several criteria were taken into consideration, including compactness, affordability, and flexibility. Following these criteria, the urban bedroom was designed as a translucent inflatable mask attached to the existing facades, facing the urban room. Each mask consists of four sleeping units, a toilet, and a corridor for circulation. The size of a mask is 10 x 10 x 6 feet plus a narrow corridor of 2 x 10 feet, with the depth depending on that of the existing apartment units. When inflated, the urban sleeper is projected into the urban room (the in-between zone); when deflated it is flush with the existing facade.

*In-between is being or occurring at an indefinite and unsettled middle place between extremes.

URBAN HOME =

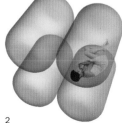

1 Translucent inflatable masks are
  attached to the facades facing the
  urban room.
2 Inflatable sleeper

2

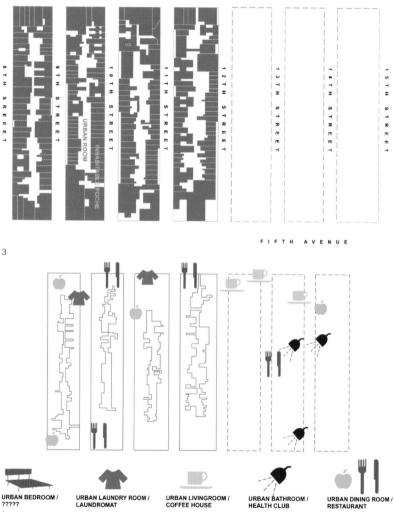

SIX AVENUE

8TH STREET

9TH STREET

URBAN ROOM

INHABITABLE POCHE

10TH STREET

11TH STREET

12TH STREET

13TH STREET

14TH STREET

15TH STREET

FIFTH AVENUE

3

URBAN BEDROOM /
?????

URBAN LAUNDRY ROOM /
LAUNDROMAT

URBAN LIVINGROOM /
COFFEE HOUSE

URBAN BATHROOM /
HEALTH CLUB

URBAN DINING ROOM /
RESTAURANT

4

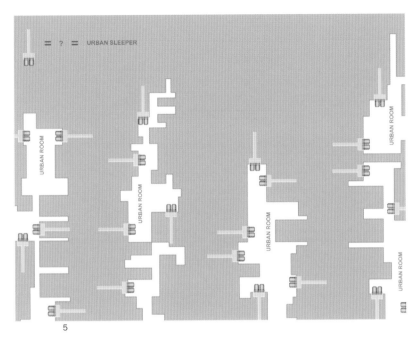

5

3 Inhabitable poché defines the "urban rooms," or the in-between space.

4 In-between living: congestion undermines the binary of the private and the public and brings about a new urban phenomenon—private activities rendered in public spaces

5 Urban sleepers inserted into urban rooms

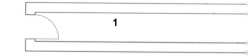

6

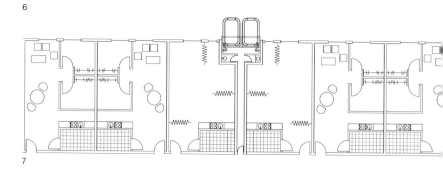

7

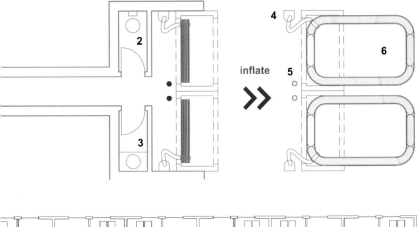

inflate

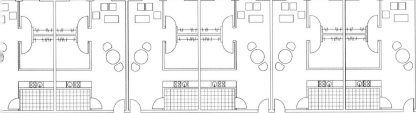

6   1: Corridor, 2: Toilet, 3: Sink, 4: Air
    pump, 5: Control button, 6: Sleeper
7   Plan

TEMPORARY PERMANENT HOUSE

In collaboration with Jr-Gang Chi

The Temporary Permanent House is envisioned as a first aid kit for natural and man-made disasters; it is a portable construction kit comprised of minimal structural and nonstructural components. The structural elements, the permanent and timeless, are standard construction parts: cross column, C-channel, tee, L-angle, and base plate. The nonstructural parts, the temporary and contingent, have shorter life cycles, which would then be replaced. These elements include an inflatable wall and roof system, stabilizing tensile chord and fasteners, plate connectors and demountable 2-x-4 flooring. Together these elements frame a 10-x-10-foot space which could then be extended over a larger area in a 10-foot module for permanent habitation.

1

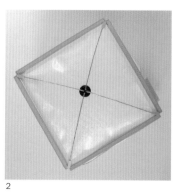

2

3

1–2 Model, roof views   3 Model, front view

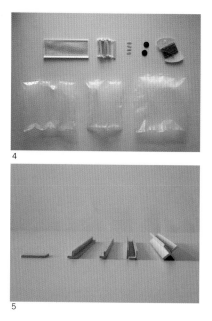

4

stabilizing tensile chord

stablilizing fastener

plate connector

5

c-channel

cross column

retractable door

demountable 2x4 flooring

floor mat

base plate

perforated door

inflatable wall

folding stair

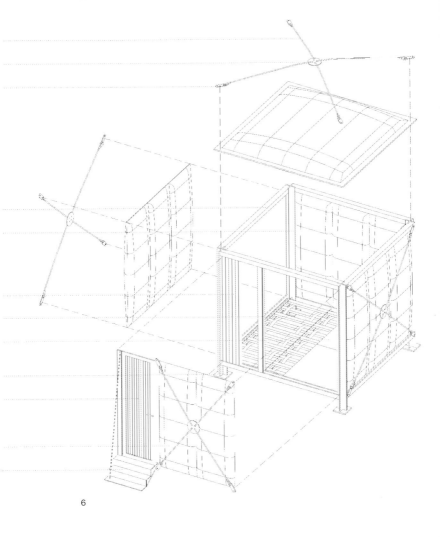

6

4 Temporary kit: inflatable wall and roof,
   stabilizing tensile chord, stabilizing fastener, plate connector, demountable
   2-x-4 flooring, perforated door
5 Permanent kit: cross column, C-channel,
   L-angle, tee, base plate

6 Explosion axon

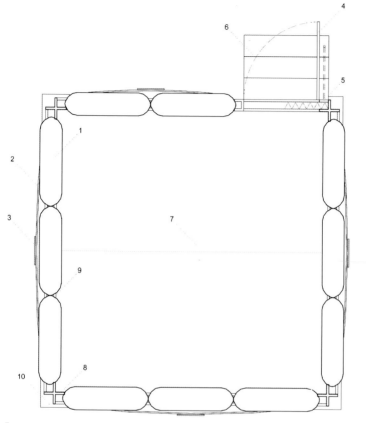

7

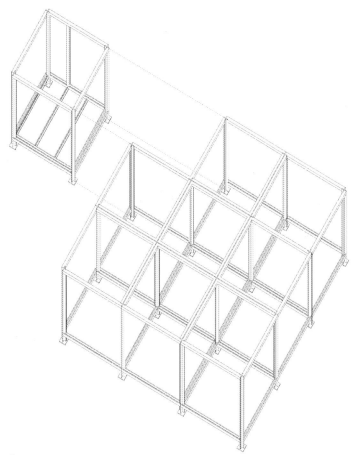

8

7 Plan: 1. inflatable wall, 2. stabilizing
   tensile chord, 3. stabilizing fasteners,
   4. perforated door, 5. retractable door,
   6. folding stair, 7. floor mat, 8. cross
   column, 9. C-channel, 10. base plate

8 The structural elements frame a 10-x-
   10-foot space, which could then be
   extended over a larger area in a 10-foot
   module for permanent habitation

ORGANIC RESTAURANT

In collaboration with Jr-Gang Chi

The organic restaurant situated among the crops is a field on a field. Together the two fields blossom during the harvest and disappear in the other seasons. When the field and restaurant blossom, their ephemeral temperament resembles that of clouds: different shapes are formed at different times; when it disappears, it leaves no traces on the field it floated upon.

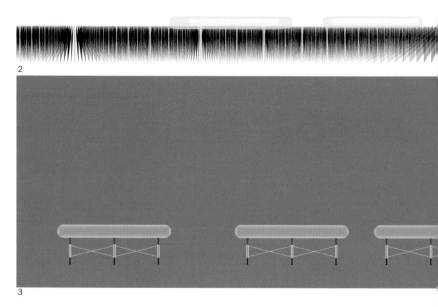

2

3

4

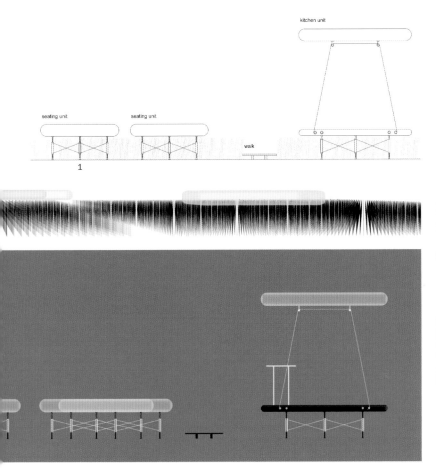

1 Seating unit and kitchen
2 Field and field
3 Elevation
4 Seating unit

N! HOUSE

What makes Argia different from other cities is that it has earth instead of air. The streets are completely filled with dirt, clay packs the rooms to the ceiling, on every stair another stairway is set in negative, over the roofs of the houses hang layers of rocky terrain like skies with clouds.

—Italo Calvino, *Invisible Cities*

The N! House aims to separate earth from air—that is, the solid from the void. It is envisioned as a series of mobile rooms in the same module— 5 x 14 1/2 x 10 feet. Each room is solid (as filled with earth), void (as with air), or an open space with landscaping. By transposing the rooms, the house can be converted into spaces for living, sleeping, and working. In theory, there are 1,662,295,315,000,320 or 24!/3x(6!) ways of rearranging the components of the house.

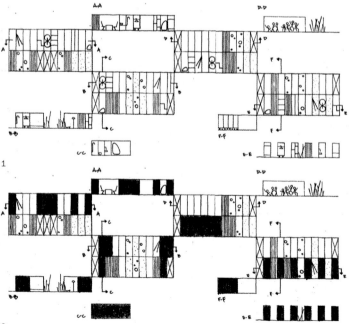

1

2

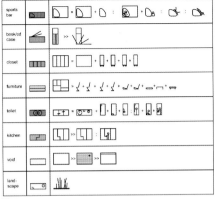

3

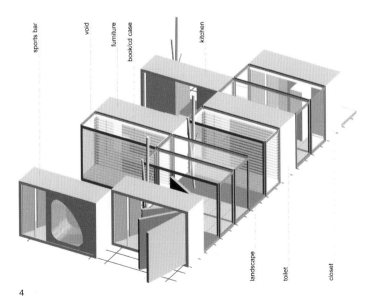

4

3 Program chart
4 Computer model

1–2 Plans and sections

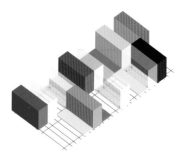

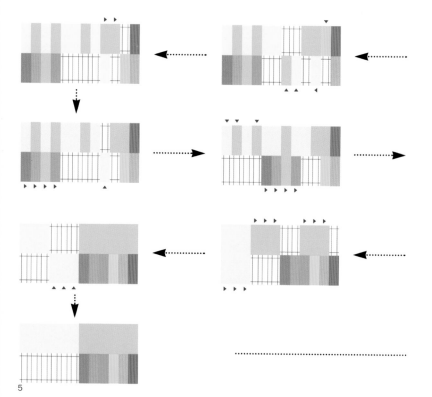

5 Sliding-tile-puzzle movement

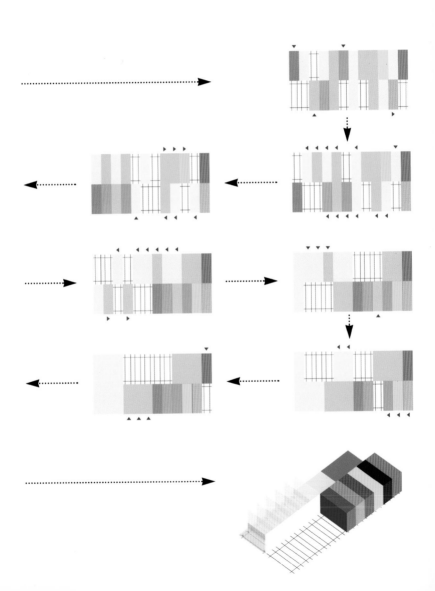

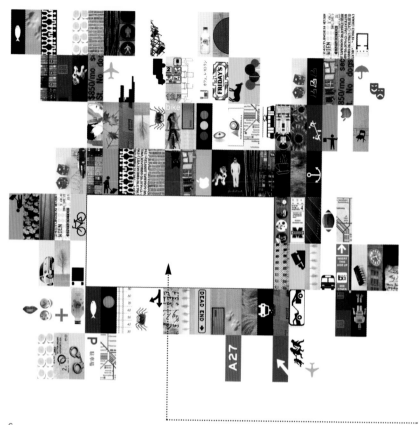

6

6 Plan: site data (left) and plan diagrams:
   continuum, divergence, quotient,
   and reciprocal
7 Solid unit 2: book/cd case; plan and
   elevation
8 Book/cd case model
9 Book/cd case model

7

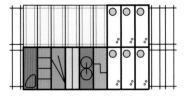

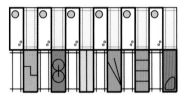

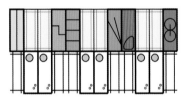

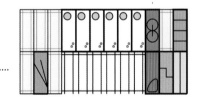

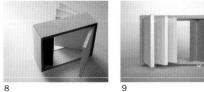

ROOM ZERO

Room Zero, the *Inhabiting Identity* installation, is a constructed manifestation of lightness.

Room Zero engages in programmatic lightness: it is intended as a place for isolation, oblivion, and erasure. Room Zero engages in functional lightness: by adjusting the density of its skin, it erases its context to different levels. Furthermore, its existence is manifested through the density of its skin. Room Zero engages in operational lightness: the time and labor required to set up Room Zero is minimal. The three steps of the installation procedure are: place the perforated panels on the floor; insert the rods into the perforated panels; slide in the tube rings through the rods. The structure is connected and supported by gravity and friction, therefore tools are not required for the installation. It takes approximately three hours for two people to assemble or disassemble the structure. Room Zero engages in material lightness: it is a structure of clear vinyl tubes and acrylic rods. These materials can be packed in boxes of 18 x 18 x 6 inches and 72 x 4 x 4 inches for shipping.

Installation credit: Jr-Gang Chi

1

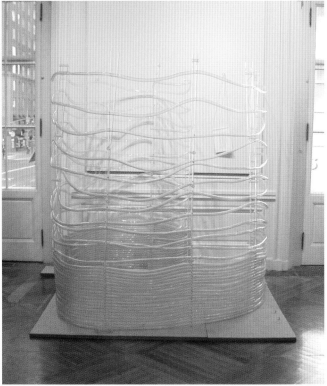

2

1 Concept sketch

2 Room Zero installation at Urban Center
Gallery, New York City

3

4

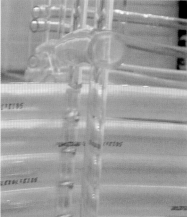

5

3 Installation procedure: 1. Place the
   perforated panels on the floor; 2. Insert
   the rods into the perforated panels; 3.
   Slide in the tube rings through the rods
4 Ring-stacking construction
5 Detail   6 Installation photo

6

STELLA BETTS

The primary focus of our work is the experience of the individual in architecture and the urban realm and how one understands and navigates one's surroundings. We investigate and strive to give form to the physical and temporal patterns inherent in a place or a site.

Our research methods include investigations of these patterns from basic understandings of site, terrain, and topography to the specific activities peculiar to a place. Our architectural production utilizes actual forms culled from research, mappings, and investigations and attempts to expose the underlying conditions within the built project: a furniture showroom can be a place to heighten the experience of viewing displayed objects by allowing them to be seen from underneath as well as from other perspectives; a lobby can be an exploration of the constant overlap of functions and movement of people in a space; a house can contain a series of conditions in a landscape that marks time as it relates to movement through a site; a city can be a laboratory for the understanding of patterns of daily life of different types of people in relation to the natural landscape they share. Rhythms and speeds in relation to occupation are revealed and examined in our work.

Seeing what is not usually seen, understanding patterns inherent in daily life, and, most importantly, enjoying the unexpectedness of these experiences, bring the inhabitant into an active relationship with our architecture. In this way we strive to locate and activate the subject in our work.

CIRCUIT SERVER

Printing Plant, New York City

This project is a printing facility in midtown Manhattan. The concept for the design was formulated as a direct response to the program. The client needed to consolidate and reorganize their space in order to improve production and to create a place where clients could review printed material. They also wanted a unique space that was unlike a typical printing plant.

Programmatically, the client's needs were twofold: first, it was necessary to have an efficient sequence of production from start to finish of a print job, meaning an easy flow of people, materials, and information from one department into another; second, all the equipment specifications had to be coordinated, such as electrical, water, and temperature control.

As we began to tackle the tasks of understanding the printing process, organizing the departments, and coordinating the layout of equipment, we realized that the project was in the specificity of the program given to us. Therefore we conceived the project as a circuit diagram where the organization of the plant was ordered around a central circulation space, and the technical necessities of equipment was laid out within a central circuit corridor. The project became a networked circulation conduit where technological and human traffic moved through this central server.

The project is located on two floors: the street level and the level below. Because half of the facility was to be located in this basement space, it was important to create an environment downstairs that did not feel oppressive and isolated. Our solution was a glowing stairwell, which functioned as the primary circulation conduit for people and information. All departments of the printing facility feed into this "server," as does the wiring that connects to the printing presses and the pre-press equipment.

The cutout for the stairwell was a 45-foot x 25-foot x 46-inch cut into the building floor plate. All movement between departments either moves directly through the glowing slot or along it. By orienting the slot of space perpendicular to the street, and by using materials that either glow with natural and artificial light or allow light and air to pass through, we were able to bring light and air deep into the facility.

Project Team: Stella Betts, David Leven; Photography: Elizabeth Felicella

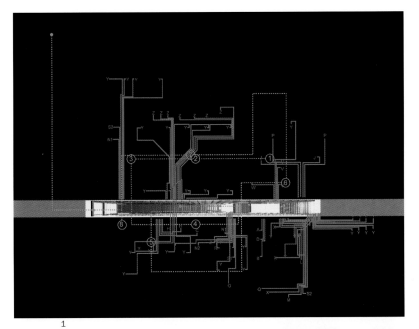

1

2   3   4

1 Circuit diagram
2 View from top of stairs; film output department at right
3 View of bridge between film output and press rooms
4 View from under stairs

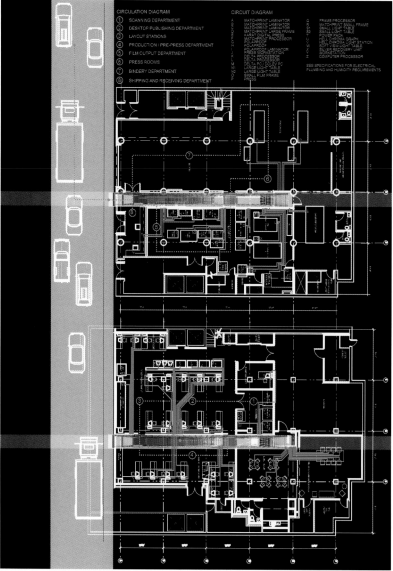

CIRCULATION DIAGRAM

① SCANNING DEPARTMENT
② DESKTOP PUBLISHING DEPARTMENT
③ LAYOUT STATIONS
④ PRODUCTION / PRE-PRESS DEPARTMENT
⑤ FILM OUTPUT DEPARTMENT
⑥ PRESS ROOMS
⑦ BINDERY DEPARTMENT
⑧ SHIPPING AND RECEIVING DEPARTMENT

CIRCUIT DIAGRAM

A   MATCHPRINT LAMINATOR
B   MATCHPRINT LAMINATOR
C   MATCHPRINT LAMINATOR
D   MATCHPRINT LARGE FRAME
E   KARAT DIGITAL PRESS
F   MATCHPRINT PROCESSOR
G   RAINAPROOF
H   POLAPROOS
I   PROCESSOR LAMINATOR
J   PRESS WORKSTATION
K   DELTA PROCESSOR
L   DELTA PROCESSOR
M   DELTA PCI / DOLEV PC
N   LARGE LIGHT TABLE
O   LARGE FILM FRAME
P   SMALL LIGHT TABLE
Q   PRESS

Q   FRAME PROCESSOR
R   MATCHPRINT SMALL FRAME
S1 SMALL LIGHT FRAME
S2 SMALL LIGHT TABLE
T   POWER PACK
U   HELL CHROMA GRAPH
V   HELL CHROMA LIGHT STATION
W   SOFT VIEW LIGHT TABLE
X   SILVER RECOVERY UNIT
Y   WORKSTATION
Z   COMPUTER PROCESSOR

SEE SPECIFICATIONS FOR ELECTRICAL
PLUMBING AND HUMIDITY REQUIREMENTS

(5) FILM OUTPUT DEPARTMENT

(4) PRODUCTION / PRE-PRESS DEPARTMENT

(2) (1) DESKTOP AND SCANNING DEPARTMENTS

VIEW FROM UNDERSIDE OF INTERSECTION BRIDGE

6

5 Plans: first floor (top), basement (below)

6 Central circulation space (above); views from underside of intersection bridge (below)

FLOOR ABOVE— CEILING BELOW

(Title from Gordon Matta-Clark: Bronx Floors, 1973)
Furniture showroom, New York City

This project is a furniture showroom in downtown Manhattan. Like the previous project, the concept for the design came directly from the program itself; we were interested in the activity of viewing and displaying that a showroom presents. The project is a series of viewing devices that utilize the placement of windows in floors and mirrors on walls to reveal the underside and multifaceted identity of the subject—whether it is the city, displayed furniture pieces, individual shoppers, or the act of the sale.

The major design intervention in this two-story showroom is comprised of three floor cutouts. These cutouts, which offer three distinct methods of furniture display, also allow views from the outside of the store and the inside, passing through the floor levels and deep into the space or back out to the street and city—depending on the position of the viewer.

Each of the three apertures is located within a floor pattern that is inscribed into the street level and sublevel of the store. At the two major termini of the pattern are mirrored panels, which reflect back toward the city and the sales desk. This simple floor pattern in the showroom is derived from a compression of the grid of the city and extends out of the store itself onto the sidewalk. The floor pattern serves as a locating apparatus not only for the cutouts but also for the visitor to the store.

The objects in the showroom are displayed on and around the three floor cutouts. Items for sale are viewable from all directions; views shoot through all spaces and levels of the store; shoppers move in relation to an inscribed path, their images reflected in mirrors at specific points; and the city is framed through the floor cutouts.

Floor cut one is located at the storefront display.
This cut is a laminated structural glass zone. The glass floor panels allow the furniture pieces displayed upon them to be viewed and inspected from below as well as from above. The cut permits the light to penetrate from the street level down into the lower

level of the showroom and workspace. At night there is a glow from the lower level of the store up onto the street.

Floor cut two is located at the stair display.
This cut has a floating acrylic display platform that allows a select few pieces to be viewed from all perspectives as one walks up or down the stairs.

Floor cut three is located at the sales desk.
This cut is a transparent and translucent sales desk. The desk slots into a cutout in the floor. It is translucent along its long faces and transparent on the top and at the two ends and holds the necessary wiring for sales equipment—the computer, credit card machine, and the telephone. One can observe the transaction occurring at the point of sale on the upper level as one moves about the objects on the lower showroom.

The idea was to create a highly orchestrated showroom experience where the visitor is an active participant in the architecture, and the exhibition of merchandise and the very act of buying and selling is on display.

Project Team: Stella Betts, David Leven; Photography: Elizabeth Felicella

1

1 Floor cut pattern diagram

2

3

4

5

6

3 Floor cut one: view under storefront display
4 Floor cut one: view under storefront display
   with office area below
5 Floor cut two: view at bottom of stairs
   under display platform
6 Floor cut three: view of sales desk

2 Floor cut one: storefront display

STEP HOUSE

Private residence, Catskills

This project is a design for a house on an eleven-acre plot of land in upstate New York. The concept for the project was derived from the site; specifically, we were interested in tracking the velocity of the landscape. The movement and direction of the slope of the land in relation to the speed of an individual on foot determined the velocity, resulting in a series of platforms. The site strategy maps a path between two points of connection (the driveway and the stream), where the house itself is one "site" on a network of platform sites.

A series of landings in the landscape enables one to negotiate the steep hill as one moves toward the stream. These landings move from the road down to the ridge, where they serve as the primary generator of form in the Step House. The land is wooded and is distinguished by this slope that begins gently, then drops off precipitously at the middle before flattening out at a wide stream that runs the full width of the property. We sited the house on the edge of this ridge, addressing the topography by stepping down to the water.

The landings are spaced in response to the rhythm of movement of an individual negotiating the slope. There are faster steps approaching the house, slower steps at the ridge at the middle and entry area of the house, and then quicker steps again as one descends down the flatter topography toward the stream.

The topography and the view to the water to the east and the orientation of the site to the sun are primary physical characteristics that the house addresses. Mostly open with glass at the first floor, the first level of the house is conceived as one of the landings in the landscape, while the second level is lifted off of the platform system and is more enclosed. This level functions as a refuge in the trees as the land falls away. The cabinetry at the first and mostly of the second level organizes the spaces and program of the house. This wood box divides the kitchen and the living area from the entry and provides coat closets at the first level, while at the second level it becomes the divider between bedrooms and the hallway, which connects all interior and exterior spaces.

Project Team: Stella Betts, David Leven, Matthew Corsover

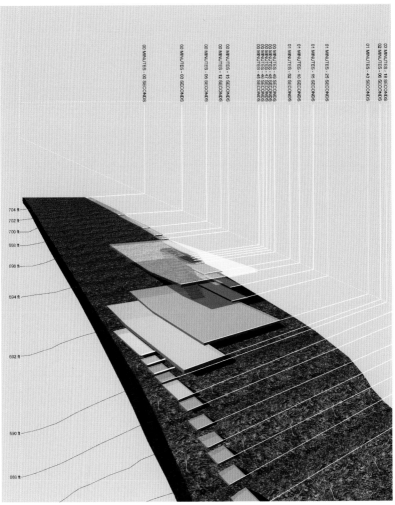

1 Site diagram

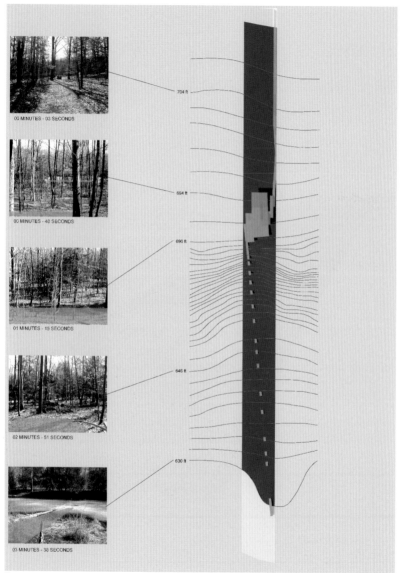

00 MINUTES - 03 SECONDS

00 MINUTES - 48 SECONDS

01 MINUTES - 15 SECONDS

02 MINUTES - 51 SECONDS

03 MINUTES - 38 SECONDS

704 ft

694 ft

690 ft

646 ft

630 ft

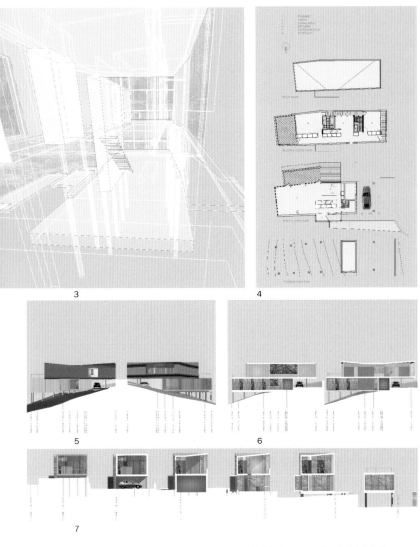

3

4

5

6

7

3 Interior perspective, looking east
4 Plans
5 North and south elevations
6 Long sections
7 Short sections

2 Site plan

REFLECTED CITY

Penthouse Apartment, New York City

This project is a penthouse apartment in New York on the twentieth floor facing north and west with views of the Empire State Building and the Chrysler Building. The concept of the project was conceived from an interpretation of the site. Since the views from the apartment were so powerful, we decided to incorporate these surrounding buildings into the site of the apartment. Therefore, the Empire State Building and the Chrysler Building would be considered as part of the domestic space of the apartment. In this instance, we were interested in the distortion of scale and distance. In order to achieve this, we developed a screen that rescales reflected images of the city into a domestic space.

The primary design element is a laminated glass wall, which functions as the image and light-capturing device. This wall is the screen that rescales reflected images of the city; it begins at the entry and runs the entire width of the apartment. The wall is slightly bent at an angle to capture reflections and to multiply the views outside, bringing them farther into the space. Moreover, the glass wall allows the qualities of light throughout the day to display on its surface the surrounding views of the city.

Project Team: Stella Betts, David Leven; Photography: Elizabeth Felicella

1

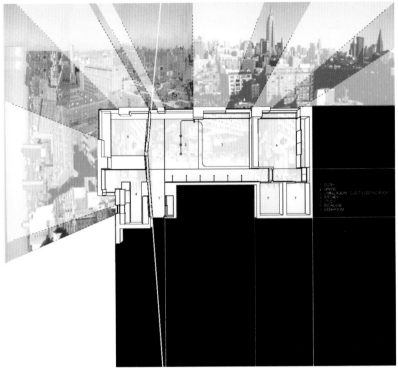

1 ENTRY
2 DINING
3 LIVING ROOM - GUEST SLEEPING ROOM
4 KITCHEN
5 WC
6 BEDROOM
7 BATHROOM

2

1 Video stills of glass wall

2 Plan showing views

3

4

5

6

8

7

9

SPACES BETWEEN THE HILLS

An urban design proposal for the region of Jerusalem-Ramallah-Bethlehem

This project is a theoretical urban design proposal for the greater region of Jerusalem-Ramallah-Bethlehem that was published in a book called *The Next Jerusalem*, edited by Michael Sorkin.

The proposal is the outcome of selective observations of the physical conditions and daily activities of the Ramalah-Jerusalem-Bethlehem region. These observations form the basis of this project, though by no means do they constitute an exhaustive study of the region's complex interplay of political, social, cultural, and religious elements.

The project begins with two investigations: one, examining the natural topography of the region and how it affects urban growth; the other charting the schedule of daily life and how that calibrates the particular temporal rhythm of the region.

The topographic analysis shows that the Ramalah-Jerusalem-Bethlehem region is profoundly shaped by two unique valley systems: one entering from the east and the other from the west. These extrude the region into a north-south linear urban formation. These natural valleys—or more specifically spaces between the hills that have functioned as the true physical borders in the region—are the sites for the proposed interventions.

As natural conditions of the landscape determine the built environment in the region, so do the confluence of the Christian, Muslim, and Jewish prayer times (representing the annual sacred cycle) frame the structure of daily life. Daily human activity occurs in the intervals between prayers—that is, between predetermined sacred times. Because the sacred schedules of the three major religions in the area are not synchronous, and because the various religious communities share the same regional space, there are overlaps and gaps where the cycle of one faith impacts the daily activities of the others. The temporal structure of the region is given largely by the staccato of daily, weekly, monthly, and yearly prayer times.

Our proposal consists of a series of suspended structures between two nodes (hills). The sites offer new territories for building within a historically and culturally "closed system." By choosing this place as the locus of our intervention and terrain for future development within the region, we hope to demonstrate the vision of the region as an integrated whole whose uppermost layer is founded not on the disputed earth but in its interstices—those which have traditionally acted as natural boundaries and defining edges separating neighborhoods and communities.

The proposal is for three sites. Each site consists of a spanning structure, which includes residential, commercial, educational, recreational, and municipal elements along with its central regional programmatic function.

Each site depicts a different architectural strategy in relation to the topographic conditions.

Project Team: Stella Betts, David Leven, David Snyder

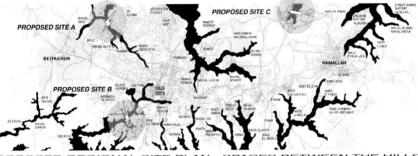

PROPOSED REGIONAL SITE PLAN - SPACES BETWEEN THE HILLS

1

1 Map of proposed site locations

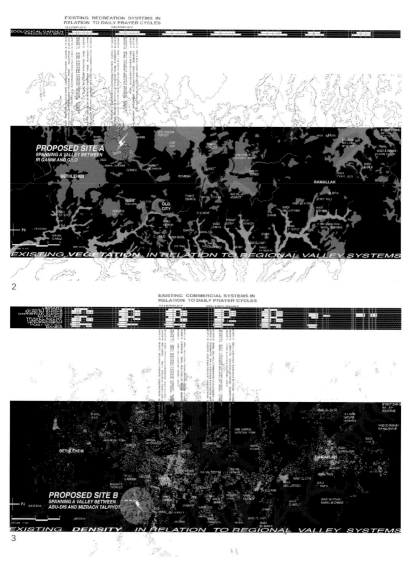

2

3

2 Existing vegetation in relation to regional valley systems (map); existing recreational systems in relation to daily prayer cycles (chart)

3 Existing density in relation to regional valley systems (map); existing commercial systems in relation to daily prayer cycles (chart)

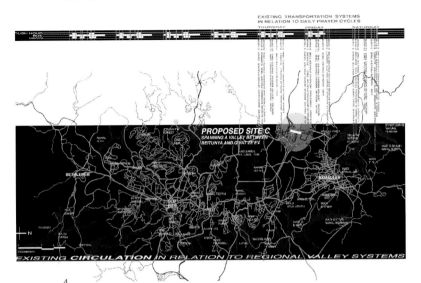

EXISTING TRANSPORTATION SYSTEMS
IN RELATION TO DAILY PRAYER CYCLES

PROPOSED SITE C
SPANNING A VALLEY BETWEEN
BEITUNYA AND GIVAT ZE'EV

EXISTING *CIRCULATION IN RELATION TO REGIONAL VALLEY SYSTEMS*

4

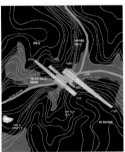

PROPOSED SITE A · RECREATIONAL SEESAW

5

PROPOSED SITE B · MUNICIPAL NECKLACE

6

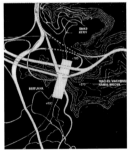

PROPOSED SITE C · TRANSPORTATION STAPLE

7

4   Existing circulation in relation to regional
    valley systems (map); existing transporta-
    tion systems in relation to daily prayer
    cycles (chart)

5   Proposed site A: recreational seesaw (a
    seesaw negotiates the topography with a
    series of ramps. The central programmat-
    ic function for this site is a recreational
    node composed of a ramping park sys-
    tem that generates the primary form and
    function of this typology.)

6   Proposed site B: municipal necklace (a
    necklace stretches across the hills sus-
    pending beaded structures. The central
    programmatic function for this site is a
    bureaucratic and municipal center com-
    posed of a series of buildings threaded
    along a major new east-west regional
    artery.)

7   Proposed site C: transportation staple (a
    staple joins the land on either side with a
    single bar. The central programmatic
    function of this site is a new transporta-
    tion hub composed of a multilayered ter-
    minal for all communication systems.)

TIME CODE

Lobby for a residential building, New York City

The design concept for this project is a tracking device for measuring the pace of movement and the activity of the individual from the street into the lobby. The time code is inscribed onto the surfaces of the architecture where individuals move "in" or "out" of time with the calibrated registration on the walls and floor.

The first element of this project is the exterior facade. Located on a pedestrian street in downtown Manhattan, the lobby for a residential apartment building reflects and frames the frenetic movement of people moving back and forth on this primary commercial strip. All of the neighboring buildings are commercial storefronts with views through to the backs of the shops.

The street presence of the lobby (the facade) acts as a reverse window in the context of the storefronts by presenting a face that allows only selected views. The lobby is set apart from the transparent street condition and therefore provides a greater degree of privacy to the tenants of the building, while affording them and the doorman framed views to the exterior as well as slices of reflected images moving through the interior of the space.

The second element of this project is the lobby itself—specifically, its rhythms and patterns of activity. The score joint arrangement in the terrazzo floor reflects these conditions and is a pattern based on the speed of an occupant and the activity being performed within the lobby. It is an inscription of one occupant at a single given time—a unit of measure. The lines in the floor continue up the adjacent walls as breaks in the glass panels in the north wall and breaks in the cement board panels in the south wall.

Inside the lobby the architectural elements track movement and cut images of people passing through. The primary element is a glass-paneled wall with horizontally sliced cutouts in front of a mirror that runs the full length of the lobby. The effect is two-fold: where the etched glass is in front of the mirror, a subtle reflection of movement is perceived; but at the cutouts where the mirror is exposed, there is a clear, cropped image of the occupant. These cutouts are located at various locations where activities occur in the lobby.

Cut 1—The Elevator Zone—is 60 to 69 inches above the floor and runs the length of the elevator vestibule. Depending on your height, you can see an upper portion of your body as you wait for or exit the elevator.

Cut 2—Bench Seating Zone—is 36 to 41 inches above the floor and runs the length of the reception area of the lobby. The height correlates to the viewline of a person seated at the bench, where they can see themselves and a midbody cut of adults or the faces and heads of children as they pass along the mirror slice.

Cut 3—Entry and Mailbox Zone—is 51 to 63 inches above the floor and runs the length of the entry, aligning with the end of the reception desk. The height allows the doorman to view the activities of the incoming residents and deliveries.

Complimentary to the slicing and marking conditions of walls and floors in the space are three horizontal planes: the first is the canopy, which runs from the outside as an illuminated weather covering through the mailbox zone and into the reception desk zone; the second is the reception desk itself; and the third is the waiting bench. Each one of these elements is set at a different height based on its function and, like the cuts in the glass wall, they create a condition of a fluid back-and-forth movement throughout the space.

Project Team: Stella Betts, David Leven; Photography: Elizabeth Felicella

1

1 Partial north elevation showing cutouts in glass wall

2

3

4

5

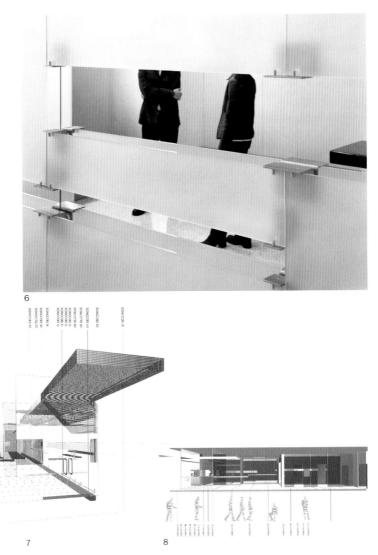

2 Entry facade
3 View to entry door
4 View toward rear
5 Clip detail at glass wall

6 Detail at glass wall
7 Lobby, score joint pattern based on time code of activity
8 South elevation showing score joint pattern

BEN CHECKWITCH

As our culture becomes increasingly immersed in all things digital, we become more concerned with the nonphysical. As such, architects today are faced with a dilemma of making material manifestations of a culture that is absorbed in the nonmaterial or virtual world. I am interested in the intersection of these two worlds, where architecture takes on the qualities of digital media and where digital media crosses over into the material world.

In many regards architects have always been in this paradoxical position relative to the physical and nonphysical. Although we are responsible for the arrangement and composition of physical materials, we rarely participate in physical construction. We operate through the abstraction of architectural representation. In contrast to working solely as an architect, I have been involved in the construction of all the built works shown here, and it is through direct experience with materials that I have learned to value them. This sentiment is most clearly demonstrated in projects like the cabin on Secret Island.

The projects that follow begin to address the relationship between the physical and digital more directly. Some projects, like the Pod, are attempts at breaking down the traditionally static nature of architecture while still operating within the language of material and form. Other projects, like the Virtual Landmark and Digital Clay, try to bring physical or corporeal qualities into the digital world. In this way, my feelings toward the potential loss of materiality in our culture could be seen as somewhat conservative, in that they try to resist the trends of the day.

CABIN

Designed as a summer getaway for a family, this small structure is on an island off the west coast of British Columbia. The building is situated close to the water while staying nestled within the trees of the densely wooded site. The focal point of the building is the view toward the open ocean to the south. Thus a directional axis is formed, starting from the entry at the north and flowing outward to this major southern vista. The building forms itself around this axis, and everything from the overall massing to the details expresses the sense of reaching out and exposing oneself to the water.

Roof beams project through to the outdoors, leading the eye toward the ocean and sky. These beams, along with the joists, the window frames, and the deck, are constructed from cedar. This cedar will initially be yellow in color, but over time will mature to a grey and match the standing seam metal roof. Ceilings and walls that extend from the inside to the outside not only blur the distinction between interior and exterior, but also provide shading devices to prevent excessive solar gain.

The house was designed in 1994 and I have since gone back to complete the first phase of construction. During this time I lived on the site and worked with a local builder and craftsman, Ian Mott.

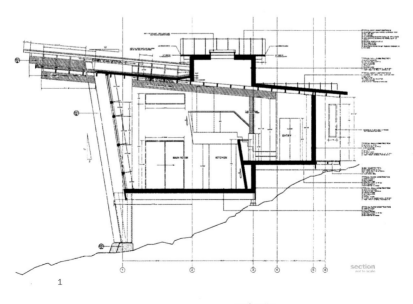

1

1 Section and plan drawing

next page:
2 Photo of model

2

3

4

5

6

7

3 Photo of model looking west
4 Photo of model looking north

5 Construction site
6 Leading edge of main platform
7 Beam, post, and footing

POD

As our perception of space becomes more fluid, adaptable, and multilayered, so does our architecture. This project rethinks the room as something that is no longer static or grounded. Designed to inhabit large, open, interior spaces, the Pod serves many purposes simultaneously: it is a lamp, a screen, a storage container, and a bedroom. It is both a piece of furniture and a piece of architecture. It is capable of holding the belongings of one individual, and as such the room can also be used as a personal moving container. It can be reconfigured to change the space in which it dwells or plug into a new one.

The Pod's walls are composed of polypropylene sheet, metal studs, and internal fluorescent fixtures. The cabinets, which also serve as doors, are upholstered in polyurethane foam, Dacron, and Lycra. Storage space is concealed beneath the bed and hidden in secret compartments in the floor/carriage. All pieces of the Pod are on casters, allowing it to roam freely within the space it inhabits.

Because this project was concerned with movement and reconfiguration, digital media—rather than print—is its preferred medium of representation. If the reader is interested in exploring this project further, please go to www.checkwitch.com/pod. Here, one will find a document that uses time and movement as an innate part of its description. In fact, this online document could be seen as the second phase of the project, as its photographs and animated line drawings are a true blend of the digital and the real.

1

2

3

4

5

1–5 Pod

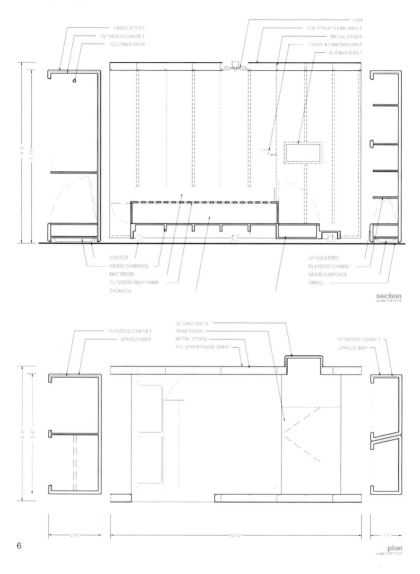

UPHOLSTERY
PLYWOOD CABINET
CLOTHES RACK

FAN
POLYPROPYLENE SHEET
METAL STUDS
LIGHT & FAN SWITCHES
SLIDING SHELF

8'-3"
7'-11"

CASTER
WOOD CARRIAGE
MATTRESS
PLYWOOD BEDFRAME
STORAGE

UPHOLSTERY
PLYWOOD CABINET
WOOD CARRIAGE
WHEEL

section
scale 1/4"=1'-0"

PLYWOOD CABINET
UPHOLSTERY

SLIDING SHELF
TRAP DOOR
METAL STUDS
POLYPROPYLENE SHEET

PLYWOOD CABINET
UPHOLSTERY

6'-2"
5'-6"

2'-6"
12'-0"

6

plan
scale 1/4"=1'-0"

6 Section and plan drawing   7–8 Pod

7

8

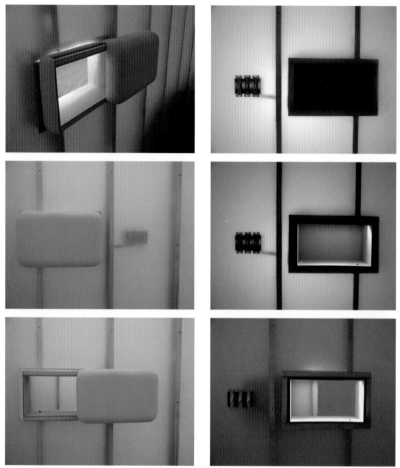

9

10

9 Sliding shelf window   10 Photomontage

FURNITURE

These two pieces of furniture were explorations in the development of a formal language that was both dynamic and mutable but also stable and grounded. The table is composed of a powder-coated steel frame that supports an acid-etched glass top. Hovering under the glass are lacquered wooden drawers mounted to the steel frame on glides. The chair is made of birch plywood, industrial felt, and piano hinges. When unfolded, its parts lock together to form a stable structure on which one can sit.

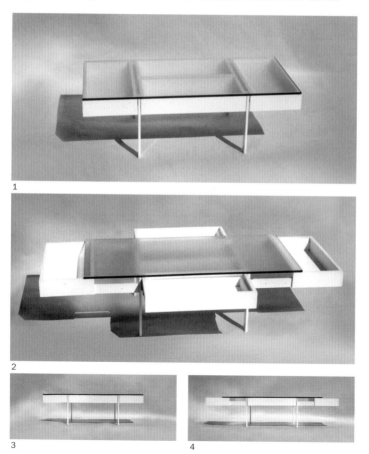

1

2

3   4

5

6   7   8   9

1 Table with drawers closed
2 Table with drawers open
3 Side view with drawers closed
4 Side view with drawers open

5 Chair unfolded
6–8 Folding chair
9 Chair, view from behind

DIGITAL LANDMARK

Located next to the Williamsburg Bridge in Brooklyn, New York, this existing building is a functioning part of the Domino Sugar Factory. This project proposes installing dimmable lights behind each of the colored glass panels. If one thinks of each window as a very large pixel, the facade can be thought of as an ultra-low-resolution computer screen. With control of the facade relinquished to web-users, the project gives a physical presence to a virtual community.

There are several ways that this installation might operate. It could be permanent or active only on specific nights or at specific times. Different dynamic light designs could be submitted and chosen by means of an on-line vote, or interface designers could control the way in which it is possible to manipulate the facade so that anyone could log on and have a place to act in the physical world.

1

2

1 View of existing Domino Sugar Factory   2 View of existing bin structure

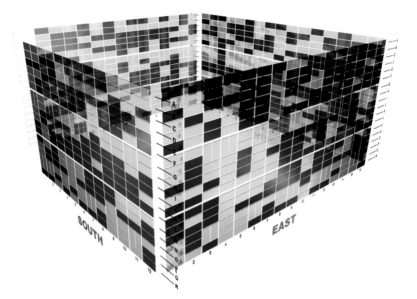

SOUTH   EAST   NORTH   WEST

3

4

5

6

7

3 Web interface   4–7 Light installation in operation

DIGITAL CLAY

If how we do things effects what we are doing, then this hypothetical tool is offered as a critique of how standard modes of human-computer interface emphasize the visual and deprive us of the corporeal. As computation seeks to separate information into discreet units (such as pixels or ones and zeros), our tactile experience with the computer has been reduced to minute touches of the fingertip. Yet our visual experience has become increasingly rich and immersive. Intended for those who digitally design physical artifacts, this tool attempts to shift the focus away from the eye and emphasize the hand as a method of work, experimentation, and play.

The mock-up shown here is composed of a 3-D matrix of points suspended in a flexible gel. Each of these points represents a capacitive sensor. If the relative distance between each point is known, then it is possible to register the manual manipulation of the tool. This can then be used to affect an entire digital model or only a small region.

Digital Clay attempts to make the interaction between hands and computers more intuitive. A simplified version of the history of architectural representation is that architects used to be builders, then abstracted building into drawing, and then drawing into CAD. This tool tries to use digital technology to reverse this process so that CAD becomes a more physical process.

1

1 Mock-up of Digital Clay

2 Digital translations of manual manipulations

manual manipulation

digital translation

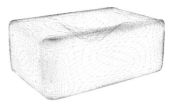

push

bend

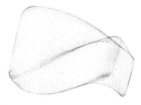

twist

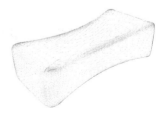

stretch

TABLE/SCREEN

This piece is an attempt at combining many of the ideas in the other projects into one. Like the previous furniture examples, it is capable of transformation. Like the Pod, it serves more than one purpose. Like the Domino Sugar Factory project, light is used as its principal medium. And like Digital Clay, it re-examines contemporary architectural representation.

Initially, the table/screen served the purpose of displaying work for the Young Architects exhibition. The gallery space, in a building designed by McKim, Mead and White, was originally a parlor room, with a mirror at one end. Using an LCD projector, computer animations and images were projected toward the mirror and then reflected back onto a screen. The screen, a 36 x 48 x 3/4-inch piece of cast acrylic, was coated with dif-fusing agents made specifically for the display of projected images.

Reconfiguring the steel armature transforms the unit into a drafting table. The screen folds down to become a desktop, and placing a mirror under the desk allows for the projection of data onto the surface of the table. In this configuration the drawing surface and computer screen are merged, allowing for a more fluid exchange between hand drawing and computer drawing.

1

2

screen configuration

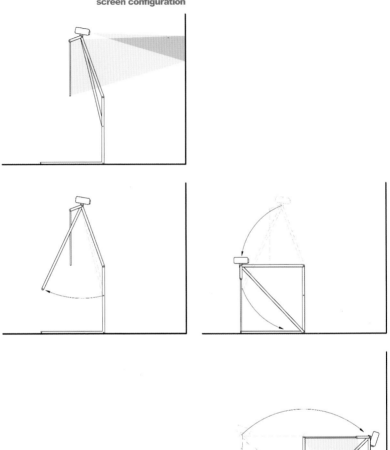

table configuration

3

1–2 Table configuration

3 Side elevations showing the transformation from screen to table

4

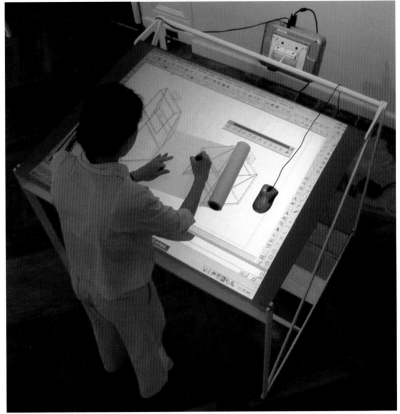

5

4 Screen configuration   5 Drafting table configuration

MIKE LATHAM

Physical manifestations of technology in contemporary life can improve the fabric and experiences of our lives. Architecture, as the way to order the elements and sociological trends around us, plays a vital role in this improvement by exposing relationships in the way that these elements and trends are constructed. Consequently, architecture aids in the understanding of the objects which are constructed, the ways in which we use them, and the reasons why we use them.

The major effects of these concerns on the work of this practice are manifested in three key areas: motion, scale, and transparency. The growing connections and similarities in space and time of the world's people, through accelerated travel and accelerated information exchange, result in the breakdown of the place-specific whole into a series of parts—pliable, reconfigureable, and fluid, like information itself. Whether at the scale of a building, furniture, an interior, or a robot, all work is made of smaller bits of information or material and is an equally compelling and challenging work of architecture. These bits are put together with a polemical, literal, and didactic transparency.

Our information-based society has accustomed the individual to look at and understand objects in new ways. Arts Corporation, as a multimedia laboratory operating at the intersections of architecture, art, and technology, is uniquely positioned to investigate, research, and construct in this highly mutable world. Our work is an attempt to reengage the individual with the work of architecture on new terms, which our technology-laden society demands. Our work moves, changes, and exchanges information.

LOFT.1

Loft.1 is a response to the overlap of different programs in a limited space. The main design element is the vitrine, a mobile glass storage space measuring 6 x 2 1/2 x 6 feet. Defined by their contents, these vitrines activate, in specific ways, the voided space that surrounds them. The space is limitlessly reconfigureable in response to changing programmatic requirements for studio, meeting, and living space. The vitrines reconfigure and recombine to take the place of walls, acting as screens. Programs flex, flow, recede, and contaminate one another. Costs are cut substantially by using this one element as wall and storage. In addition, permanent improvement costs in a leased space are avoided. Glass contributes to the openness and movement of light through a long space where some areas are 70 feet from a window.

Photography: Andrew Bordwin

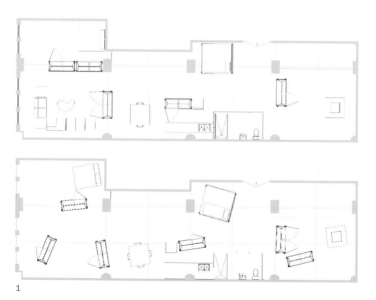

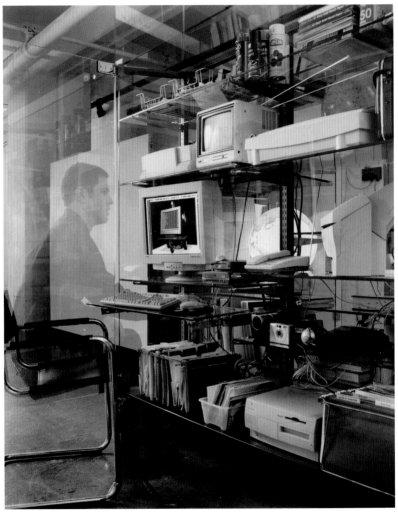

2

2 The Study. The vitrines have uniform exterior measurements, but standards on the interior are adjustable at increments of 1 inch, allowing for great variation in function.

1 The plan is limitlessly reconfigureable.

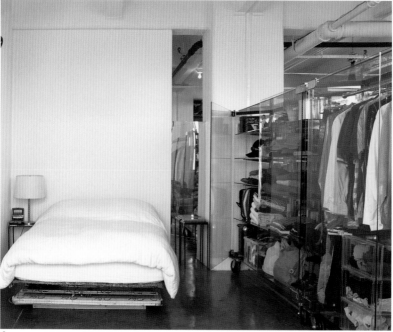

3

4

4 Vitrines create a moving wall, separating
   a bedroom from a living area.

5

5 Like the vitrine, CUBE is fully mobile.

6

7

5–7 The guest box serves as guest room,
light fixture, art installation, and storage
space for large objects. One side
remains open for access; the box can
be completed with any existing station-
ary wall. The opposite side is made
of a two-way mirror which protects the
fluorescent fixtures but allows for privacy
when turned off.

HOME.IN.1

Home.in.1 had a limited budget for the creation of storage space and furniture—a bed, bookshelves, and a desk—in a New York studio space. The client expressed dissatisfaction with her seemingly interminable series of rented apartments, a reluctance to spend money in a space where she could not predict how long she would stay, and a desire to create a sense of "home" despite these circumstances. The solution conflates the furniture program and the client's possessions in a mobile six-foot cube or pixel made of standard 1 1/4-inch shelving angles, glass, and acrylic. In its photographed location, the result is an open and organized space, which might otherwise be overwhelmed by objects. The cube and all of its contents can be moved against a wall allowing for open studio work space. The unit can be disassembled and reassembled by two people in two days. The cube becomes the home; where that home resides is of less importance. The cube and its owner currently reside in Las Vegas, NV.

Photography: Andrew Bordwin

1

2

3

1 Plan of the Brooklyn location,
  March 2001 through August 2002
2 The front section of a prefab aluminum
  ladder is the means of access to the
  lofted bed.

3 Mission Control: electricity is provided
  to the desk and night stand area (not
  shown). The glass desk and shelves
  rest on the standard 1 1/4-inch steel
  angles.

4

4 Fluorescent bulbs are incorporated into
the interior of the structure. When off,
the cube assumes a serene white
appearance. When on, light and color
permeate the translucent acrylic.

5 Exterior doors allow access to the desk,
bookshelves, closet, and the ladder to
the bed above.

6 You are always Home.

5

6

BRIDGE

The overstructured steel towers of early twentieth-century bridges are harbingers of the modern skyscraper, or skyscrapers before they are coated in their curtain walls. The Williamsburg neighborhood in Brooklyn, New York, has for many years been a center of the conversion of disused industrial buildings into live/work space for the arts community. As real estate prices rise, every last recess of the city is candidate for colonization. Williamsburg Bridge Lofts take these eventualities one step further by proposing to fill out the empty spans of the bridge tower with city-subsidized lofts of between 900 and 1,500 square feet. In effect building on what is now fallow city-owned land. The missing curtain wall is reinstated in a flexible, pliable form.

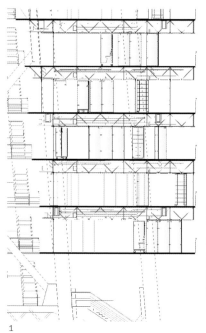

1

2

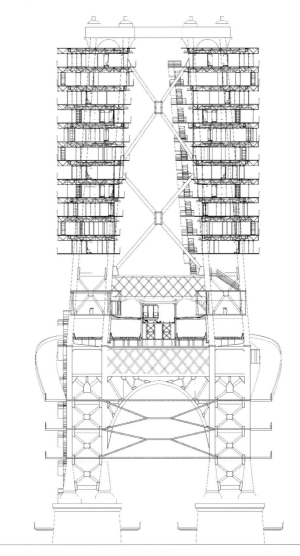

3

1 Section through five lofts, all with
   variant floor plans from the identical kit
   of parts
2 The Brooklyn tower

3 Section of the tower structure showing
   parking garage (added, bottom), road
   and train levels (existing, middle), lobby
   (added, above road), and eleven-
   story loft addition (top)

4

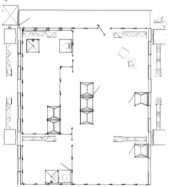

5

6

7

4 The size of outdoor spaces is adjustable partly in response to seasonal variations.
5 Plan for winter
6 Plan for summer

7 Both the mobile shower unit and the mobile toilet unit have a Polyvision film insert, which becomes opaque when charged with electricity. The units are alternately private bathing spaces and sculpture. Plumbing is supplied through flexible polyurethane piping attached via quick disconnect at nine gridded wet stations.

8

8 Storage cabinets are mounted with ball
bearings to the 3-foot gridded space
frame, so their position is adjustable.
A combination of translucent and transparent glasses allow for varying degrees
of privacy. As storage cabinets fill up
with possessions, they become opaque
walls, and the space is personalized.

HAYDEN HALL

Hayden Hall is a project for the interior renovation of a New York single-room occupancy (SRO) into a boutique hotel aimed at a young clientele. The directive includes refurbishment and furniture for eighty-two rooms (about half with en suite bath), expansion of the lobby area, and the creation of a bar in the basement space under the lobby. The eight-story building, constructed in 1902, shows the history of its years of use. Rather than stripping and remodeling, and in light of the budget (under forty dollars per square foot), there is a dual strategy of concealing and revealing. Rough walls with peeling paint are covered in flat sheet rock. Architectural features such as moldings and windows are, however, left untouched, framed by the new additions and left as highly textured installations, which show the history of the building. Furniture is approached as a limited series of high-impact installations.

1 Section, bar and lobby at bottom,
   "light" shaft at right

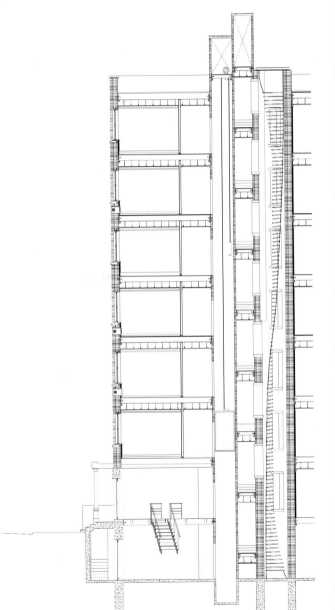

1

2

3

4

5

2 The glass bar is the main element of
the basement design. Fenestrations are
removed and replaced with glass panes.

3 The "light" shaft installation, at the
heart of the building, unifies the experience of the building. Fluorescent bulbs
keyed to the front desk run 94 feet
from the basement bar to the roof, and
switch on or off in response to room
occupancy. Updated life safety systems
allow the shaft to be capped with a sky-
light and the removal of the windows.

4 The hallway lighting scheme is devised
to highlight the retained architectural
detail, including doors and moldings.
Bulbs are recessed in soffets behind
new sheet rock.

5 A glass stair, in orientation and material
expressive of its newness, connects
the bar and the lobby, where the floor
has a thick polyurethane coat over the
original baseboards and raw concrete
where walls have been removed. The
front desk key system is keyed to the
light installation in the air shaft.

FIELD HOUSE

In the foothills of the Catskill Mountains in northern Pennsylvania, rock ledge lies an average of 4 feet beneath the ground surface, and fresh, warm water aquifers, which lie about 75 feet below the surface, feed trout streams. Besides being known as the land of heart-shaped Jacuzzis and beautiful Mt. Airy Lodge, this area is also known for its concrete factories and trout streams. Field House serves as a prototype, both as a seminal investigation in cooperation with Paul Ochs and A.C. Miller Concrete, a regional concrete producer, into the feasibility of mass-produced precast concrete homes and as the first in a development of several homes for casual, vacation living on large pieces of property with spectacular views of the Catskill mountains. In deference to this pristine setting and economic realities (some of the houses are as much as a mile from an existing power line), the design of the houses emphasizes self and environmental sustainability. Despite an open front wall of glass, high insulation value is maintained throughout the house with the help of features such as a garden roof, which restores the landscape covered by the footprint of the house and provides deer-free gardening space. The house is powered off-the-grid by a propane generator and solar cells and is heated through radiant slabs by geothermal means.

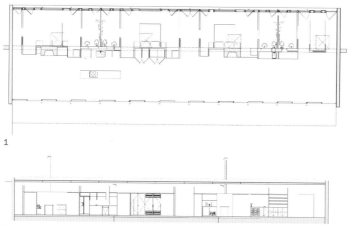

1

2

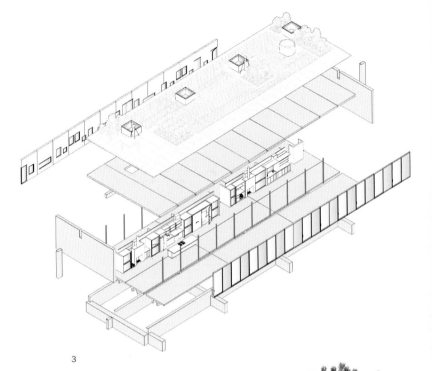

3

1 Plan
2 Section, showing the highly elaborated
  core
4 The only customized piece of the house
  is the central core. Conceived as a
  sculpture inside the prefabricated box,
  it houses all of the functional components and divides the living area from
  the bedrooms. The house is assembled
  like a contemporary kit of parts, resulting in substantial cost savings.

next page:
5 Field House sits at the top of a large
  field with a sixty-mile view from its front
  side. Glass sliding doors make up the
  front side.

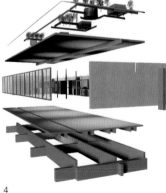

4

END